CARE, DARE, SHARE, BE FAIR

The Story of IBA

CARE, DARE, SHARE, BE FAIR

The Story of IBA

Nicolas Coupain

Lannoo

FOREWORDS

It's difficult to imagine being the parent of a thirteen-month-old with cancer.

When we went to the hospital, we discovered what we already suspected: a brain tumor. More precisely, an AT/RT tumor—one of the most aggressive types out there. When the doctors mentioned the possibility of radiation therapy, our response was immediate: "No."

We'd heard about proton therapy but weren't sure if it was right for Viggo. We were shocked and felt it was incredibly unfair that such a promising technology wasn't available in Belgium. So, we took matters into our own hands and reached out to the Paul Scherrer Institute in Switzerland.

What mattered most was that Viggo maintained a good quality of life. In 2012, the benefits of proton therapy were not yet fully confirmed, but Swiss doctors mentioned survival rates of 60 to 70 percent, whereas statistics for an AT/RT tumor showed only 10 to 15 percent in the first year. With approval from our healthcare system, we traveled to Switzerland for nine weeks.

We were lucky—but this should be guaranteed. Every parent should have access to this option without having to struggle alone. Luckily, we had support: coworkers, friends, and family stood by us. When they asked how they could help, we told them: "Talk about proton therapy."

For us, proton therapy was a lifeline. Once the treatment started, hope came back. How many children could have had the same chance? How many had to settle for a less suitable treatment simply because the best option wasn't available?

Today, fourteen years later, Viggo is doing well. He was bilingual by age four; his IQ is above average; his education and development are completely typical. Today, we believe that none of this would have been possible without proton therapy.

Our testimony is that of a family—but also a plea to make this treatment accessible to everyone. Because Viggo should not be an exception.

- Steve & Valérie Mommaerts,
Viggo's parents

Long before I walked the corridors of Massachusetts General Hospital as a faculty member, I was sending my patients here.

For decades, working as a radiation oncologist at the University of California, San Francisco (UCSF), I encountered cases where the limits of conventional radiation were too consequential to accept. Whether a child with a brain tumor or an adult with a spinal cord tumor, I referred my patients to MGH, knowing and trusting that they would receive exceptional, unrivaled care.

In 2015, I joined the Harvard Radiation Oncology community and every experience here, every day, confirmed all that I had understood from a distance.

Proton therapy has transformed the way we think about radiation. Because protons deposit their energy at a precise, controllable depth, they can be targeted with an accuracy that conventional radiation cannot match. Tumors near critical structures—spinal cord, optic nerves, developing brain of children—these have been patients for whom proton therapy did not merely improve outcomes. It transformed them.

In the years since, we have treated thousands of patients at MGH. What we have witnessed, again and again, is not only survival, but also preserved quality of life. Children who finished school. Adults who returned to work. Families spared the long shadow of late effects. These outcomes are not incidental. They are the purpose. They are the vision.

This book marks forty years of a field that dared to ask: what if we could do better? The answer required physicists, engineers, clinicians, and institutions to work in concert. The history of proton therapy is, at its core, a story of collective ambition.

The work is far from over. The gap between what is scientifically possible and what is available to patients remains too wide. Too many children still receive treatments less precise than what we know is achievable. Closing that gap is not a commercial question. It is a moral one.

- Daphne Haas-Kogan, MD Professor, Harvard Medical School | Department of Radiation Oncology, Massachusetts General Hospital (MGH)

TABLE OF CONTENTS

IBA treats cancer by setting up proton therapy centers and developing therapeutic radioisotopes.

INTRODUCTION

Boston, November 7, 2001. In a treatment room at Massachusetts General Hospital, a patient takes a decisive step in the fight against cancer, becoming the first person in the world to receive proton therapy delivered using a technology developed by a small company—one founded just fifteen years earlier in a university laboratory in Louvain-la-Neuve, Belgium. At once intimate and universal, this moment captures the very essence of IBA's journey: transforming bold scientific ideas into innovations that save lives. For the engineers, physicians, and entrepreneurs who dedicated years to realizing this vision, it signified far more than a technical or commercial achievement. It stood as living proof that the improbable can indeed become reality.

Since the delivery of this first life-saving proton beam, IBA has become the undisputed leader in proton therapy, with approximately half of all patients treated worldwide receiving care on its systems. Yet significant barriers remain for many patients who could benefit from this technology. Viggo, pictured on the cover as a young child, was among the fortunate. In 2012, at the age of one, he received a decisive course of treatment in Switzerland—care that enabled him to grow up like any other child. While IBA did not build this machine, the company worked tirelessly alongside Viggo's family in the fight to improve access to proton therapy.

IBA uses radioisotopes produced
by its cyclotrons and chemical equipment
to improve the accuracy of diagnoses.

These efforts, like many others described in the pages that follow, are part of a trajectory shaped by four guiding principles that IBA formalized in 2004 after a period of deep introspection: *care*, *dare*, *share*, and *be fair*. These core values resonate throughout IBA's history.

CARE relates to the clinical mission: patients, safety, quality, the well-being of team members, and their impact on the world.

DARE embodies technological courage, non-linear approaches, and a creative drive that rejects the idea that "we've always done it this way."

SHARE suggests an open ecosystem, the flow of knowledge, and the sharing of collective achievements.

BE FAIR reflects balanced governance, reciprocity, and the pursuit of the common good.

These ideals are not fixed doctrines but sources of inspiration, continually tested by reality. Together, they form a framework that must be constantly reexamined and reinvented to sustain dialogue between science, medicine, and industry.

IBA's history has been shaped by both progress and setbacks—through leaps forward, unforeseen crises, and the need to rebuild balances repeatedly. This book invites readers to explore that journey and the philosophy behind it, illustrating how these values have been embodied—and sometimes challenged—by real-world situations. The aim is twofold: to preserve memory, ensuring the origins, choices, doubts, failures, and achievements that define IBA are not forgotten, and to shed light on the future by providing reference points for navigating an increasingly complex world.

IBA guarantees the quality
and precision of care delivered through
its dosimetry solutions.

The first part of this book traces IBA's journey while addressing a series of fundamental questions. How can ongoing innovation act as both a driver of growth and a necessity for survival in the most demanding areas of medical technology? How far can audacity be pushed without compromising the organization's integrity? How can mission and profitability be balanced? How can strong values be maintained when crises threaten to undermine everything? How can local roots and stable ownership support a global ambition? How did an SME founded in a university laboratory manage to bring together such a remarkable pool of talent around a distinct culture? And perhaps most challenging of all, how can time be managed—responding swiftly to customer expectations while building a resilient model?

The second part of this book examines IBA's philosophy: the principles that inspired its successive leaders, the development of its corporate culture from a technology start-up to an international group, and how the company's history prepares it for the future. How can a company like IBA maximize its positive contribution to society? What lessons has IBA learned from its past that will allow it to become an increasingly resilient and successful organization in the years ahead? Reflecting on decisions made, achievements realized, and challenges surmounted, a set of common themes appears. These constants are not just keys to understanding the past; they also act as compasses for navigating the future.

But before exploring this twofold narrative—encompassing both historical account and philosophical reflection—it is worth recalling its purpose. What is the point of these ion beams, gigantic magnets, and years of relentless research? IBA's particle accelerators serve four vital functions: diagnosing, treating, monitoring, and protecting.

IBA protects life by sterilizing medical devices with its Rhodotron-based irradiation solutions.

Diagnosis, first. Through IBA's radiopharmaceutical solutions, millions of patients each year benefit from more accurate diagnoses in oncology, cardiology, and neurology. The isotopes produced enable earlier detection of cancer, cardiovascular conditions, and neurodegenerative diseases, helping physicians to see, monitor, and anticipate.

Treatment, second. IBA's technologies enable the precise targeting of tumors with unparalleled precision while sparing healthy tissue. Each proton therapy center represents a promise: safer, more targeted, and more patient centered care. Treatment is no longer limited to proton therapy. IBA's accelerators also produce radioisotopes used in theranostics, an emerging approach that combines diagnosis and treatment within a single clinical pathway.

Control, constant. Precision lies at the heart of IBA's mission. Through dosimetry, the company guarantees that every dose delivered—both for imaging and treatment—is exactly as prescribed. By making the invisible visible, IBA safeguards quality.

Protect, always. By adapting its technologies to industrial needs, IBA contributes to the sterilization of medical devices, the improvement of materials, and the reduction of environmental impact. It is a discreet yet decisive contribution to the safety and quality of everyday life.

Over the decades, these applications have been refined and honed around a single guiding principle: applying the engineering of physics in the service of life.

This account is based on thorough research using both internal and external archives. It is shaped by many testimonials from those who contributed to the company's success. While not all can be named, none are forgotten. They are all acknowledged here with gratitude. Behind every technology, there are people; behind every patient treated, there is a story.

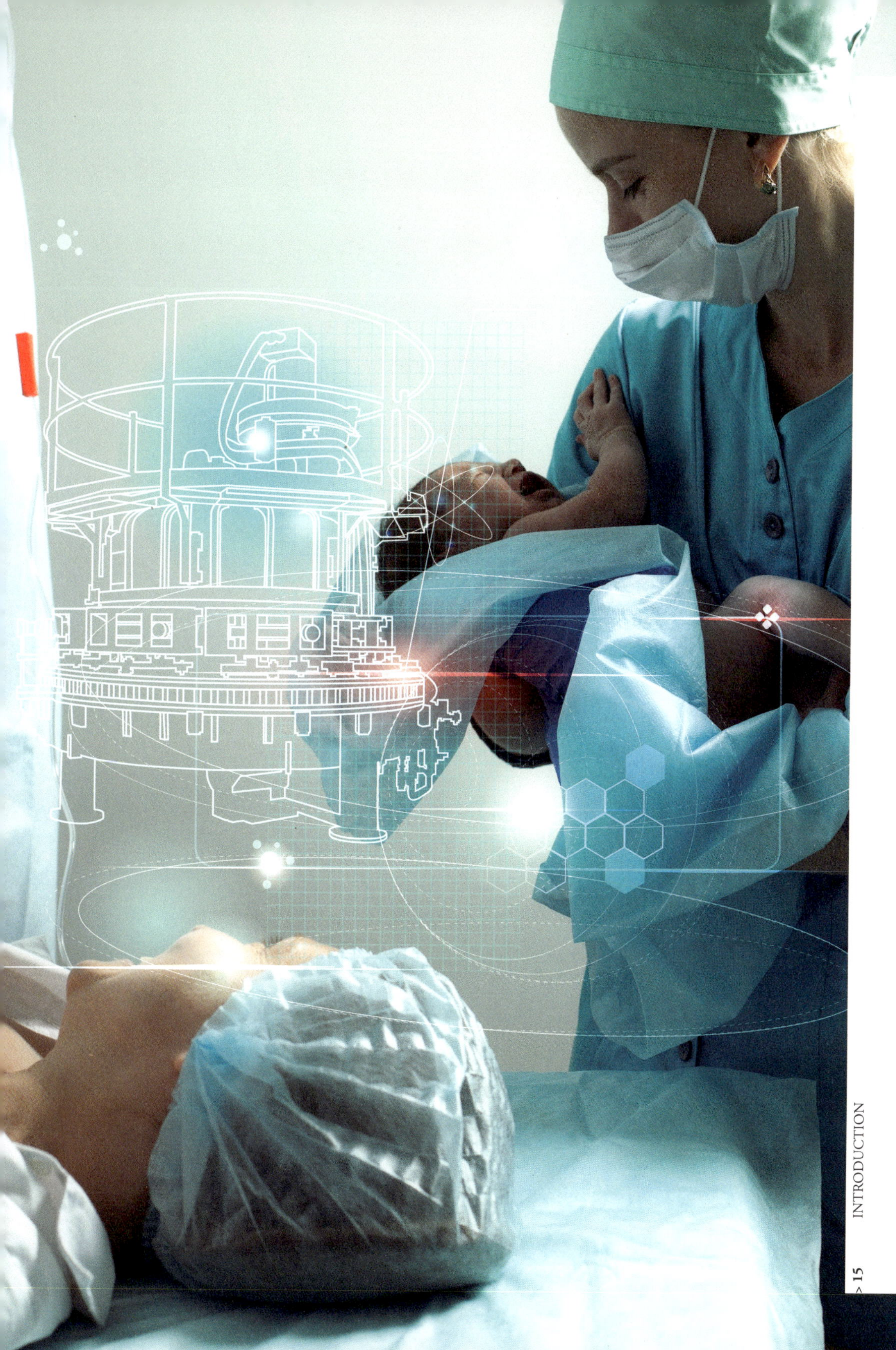

ACCELERATORS TO SAVE LIVES: THE EPIC STORY OF IBA

I

Installation of an IBA cyclotron at Belgium's first proton therapy center at the hospital in Leuven, Belgium, 2019.

A STAR IS BORN

[1986-1987]

1

The Lawrence Berkeley National Laboratory, overlooking San Francisco Bay, where Yves Jongen envisioned the industrial potential of university cyclotrons.

The spark

California, November 18, 1983. From the hilltop overlooking San Francisco Bay where the Lawrence Berkeley National Laboratory stands, Yves Jongen, 36, took in the view. After nearly fourteen years as director of the Cyclotron Research Center (CRC) in Louvain-la-Neuve, he was spending a sabbatical in what was then considered the main center for cyclotron research. He had been invited to install an electron-cyclotron resonance (ECR) ion source developed for the first time in Louvain-la-Neuve. The source had attracted the attention of American researchers and was meant to produce high-intensity ion beams for experiments in fundamental nuclear physics. Yves would later describe this period as one of the most productive of his scientific career. His days were filled with discussions with colleagues, his nights with solitary work in the deserted laboratory. He regularly surprised his American peers with the speed at which he developed several complex devices.

Taking advantage of this stimulating intellectual atmosphere and this change of playing field, he spent that evening reflecting on the future course of his career. Gradually, a conviction took hold: the heyday of the cyclotron as a basic tool for fundamental research in physics was drawing to a close. Many laboratories were abandoning nuclear physics in favor of particle physics, which was more in vogue. The time seemed to have come to design cyclotrons better suited to industrial use, with applications intended to benefit the greatest number of people. What if these tools of the infinitely small could protect, improve, and save the infinitely precious—human life?

The intuition that sparked Yves Jongen's mind in the fall of 1983 was the result of the convergence of a major scientific field and the trajectory of a man firmly established in the microcosm of accelerator experts.

"Every time
a physicist accelerates
a new type of beam,
doctors wonder
what they
can do with it."

- Yves Jongen

Cyclo… what?!

Since the 1930s, particle accelerators have been essential tools for fundamental research in nuclear and particle physics, uniquely capable of experimentally demonstrating the brilliant theoretical concepts of the greatest scientists in History. These accelerators were created to propel charged particles—such as electrons, protons, and ions—to very high speeds, often nearing the speed of light, thus giving them substantial kinetic energy. Their fundamental principle involves using electric fields to accelerate particles and magnetic fields to steer and focus them. Unlike nuclear reactors, which can spiral out of control if not properly managed, particle accelerators are electrical devices that can be stopped instantly by simply cutting off their power supply. Today, more than 50,000 accelerators are in operation worldwide, ranging from small to large, and are used in scientific, medical, and industrial applications.[1]

The origins of particle accelerators date back to the early twentieth century, beginning with the first experiments on atomic structure. By bombarding gold foil with alpha particles emitted by radioactive substances, Ernest Rutherford confirmed the existence of the atomic nucleus. These experiments highlighted the need for higher-energy projectiles to explore matter more thoroughly, leading to the development of increasingly advanced artificial methods for accelerating particles. After reading a pioneering article by the Norwegian physicist Rolf Widerøe, Ernest O. Lawrence and his student Milton S. Livingston built the first functional prototype of a cyclotron in Berkeley in 1930. This initial cyclotron had a diameter of only a few centimeters and could accelerate protons to 80 kiloelectronvolts (keV). It earned Lawrence the Nobel Prize in Physics in 1939. Lawrence quickly improved the design of his device, constructing larger and more powerful machines and paving the way for "Big Science". The last cyclotron built under his direction, from 1958 onward—the "88-inch" cyclotron, which is still in operation today—was the one on which Yves Jongen installed a new electron-cyclotron resonance (ECR) ion source inspired by the device developed in Belgium.[2]

Standard cyclotrons were circular accelerators where an oscillating electric field pushed charged particles in a spiral, while a steady magnetic field kept them on a circular path. However, these devices soon faced limitations as particles reached relativistic speeds. To overcome this energy barrier, various innovations appeared: the synchrotron, which varies the magnetic field and frequency to keep particles in a stable orbit; the synchrocyclotron, which decreases the acceleration frequency as the particles' mass increases; and the isochronous cyclotron, which maintains a constant frequency by adjusting the magnetic field to focus the beam. The Catholic University of Louvain (UCL) installed this final type of cyclotron in the early 1970s.

The core of Belgium's first cyclotron in Leuven, on display in Louvain-la-Neuve.

King Baudouin with Yves Jongen (right) during the UCL foundation stone laying ceremony at the Cyclotron Research Center in Louvain-la-Neuve, 1971.

The atom of national discord

At the same time that Ernest Lawrence began designing the first cyclotron in Berkeley, Ghent born Marc de Hemptinne was appointed professor of physics at the University of Louvain. A pioneer of molecular spectroscopy, he was driven by a single ambition: to endow his *alma mater* with a department of experimental physics. The two men met in Berkeley in 1938. Upon his return to Belgium, Marc de Hemptinne set himself the goal of installing a cyclotron at the still-unified Catholic University of Louvain to produce radioactive atoms for the study of molecular structure.[3] Interrupted by the war, the project came to fruition in 1947 thanks to subsidies from the Interuniversity Institute of Nuclear Physics (IIPN), which he chaired, and to sponsorship from the Union Minière du Haut Katanga. The sale of uranium extracted in the Congo to the United States by Belgian industrial groups significantly accelerated the development of Belgium's nuclear sector and, indirectly, that of applied and fundamental research.[4] In 1952, the Centre for the Study of Nuclear Energy Applications (CEAEN) was established. It was later relocated to Mol, near Belgium's first nuclear reactor, and renamed SCK-CEN.[5] Through the convergence of industrial enterprises—electrical, mechanical, and steelmaking—outstanding university research centers, and a committed public policy, the Belgian ecosystem reached the forefront of expertise in civil nuclear energy. In this context, one of the major contributions of the Louvain cyclotron was enabling the formation of a dynamic team of young physicists and fostering close collaboration with chemists and physicians.[6] This rapprochement, which later proved fundamental to IBA's history, took root at this early stage.

COEUR DU 1er CYCLOTRON BELGE
1947

As the linguistic conflict between Flemish and Walloons escalated in late 1965, plans to create a French-speaking section of the UCL in Walloon Brabant and Brussels gained momentum. In parallel, a new project for a 100-megavolt (MeV) isochronous cyclotron was launched, driven by the influential Marc de Hemptinne and his disciple and successor, Pierre Macq—the future rector—who also returned from a year of study at the Berkeley laboratory.[7] The new cyclotron was to be built on the Lauzelle plateau, demonstrating UCL's commitment to establishing itself in Wallonia. At the time, several industrial companies were manufacturing custom cyclotrons for university research—primarily to build prestige rather than for financial gain—including Siemens in Germany, Philips in the Netherlands, and Thomson CSF in France. The latter was chosen to design the machine. The Charleroi Electrical Construction Workshops (Ateliers de Constructions Électriques de Charleroi, ACEC) produced most of the mechanical components and electronic parts.

On February 2, 1971, surrounded by thirteen of his ministers and representatives from thirty countries, King Baudouin attended the laying of the foundation stone for the Catholic University of Louvain during a ceremony held in the grand hall of the cyclotron in Louvain-la-Neuve. That same year, the Institut National des Radioéléments (IRE) was established in Fleurus, in the Charleroi region, which was then seeking industrial reconversion. Led by René Constant, the IRE aimed to become the Walloon counterpart of SCK-CEN, primarily involved in producing radioisotopes for medical applications. Thus, applied nuclear physics took hold in the Walloon Region, marking the start of a path that would support the creation and growth of IBA. In 1972, CYCLONE (CYClotron de LOuvain-la-NEuve) produced its first beams under the guidance of Yves Jongen. The man later nicknamed "the first inhabitant of Louvain-la-Neuve", who regularly wore rubber boots to cope with the ever-present mud of the city under construction, was appointed as the technical manager of the Cyclotron Research Center (CRC)—in the absence of a more experienced candidate.

Yves Jongen: A life at 643 million km/h[8]

Raised in Nivelles, in Walloon Brabant, and the son of radiologist Robert Jongen, Yves was close to completing a double degree in electronics and physics at what was then called "Louvain-l'ancienne" (Old Leuven). In the course of his studies, he developed a close relationship with Pierre Macq, who became his mentor. Macq was impressed by Yves's ingenuity during an internship, where he successfully demonstrated the potential of a prototype detector entrusted to the university laboratory. Yves also held numerous discussions with his professor about the best way to steer his engineering career toward technology. During visits to various factories, Yves observed that engineers tended to move quickly into management roles, distancing themselves from practical work to handle meetings and bureaucratic constraints. This prospect appealed to him "about as much as breaking rocks in a penitentiary", as he later wrote.[9] Macq himself had faced a similar dilemma. Urged by his father to take over the family electronics business, he had instead chosen to interrupt his engineering studies and redirect his career toward physics. Rather than advising Yves to follow the same path, he encouraged him to persevere, stating: "Physics research needs good engineers, and there are complementary studies in physics".[10]

Yves was close to completing his double degree when he learned of an opening for the position at the CRC he scarcely dared to envision. As the word "impossible" was not part of his vocabulary, he confided in Pierre Macq about his ambition and submitted his application. Published in CERN's newsletter and other leading scientific journals, the job posting called for ten years of experience in managing a large accelerator. However, specialists were rare and highly sought after to lead other centers then under development around the world. Convinced of his student's talent and motivation, Pierre Macq made the bold decision to support his application, much to the skepticism of his colleagues, who believed he had lost his mind.

Thus, Yves secured a position commensurate with his aspirations, even before graduating. This personal experience would later inspire him to entrust young colleagues with significant responsibilities. He would also make sure that technical careers were valued as highly as managerial positions.

A new world opened up to him. The pace was intense. To cope with the increasing workload, Yves hired an assistant, Guido Ryckewaert, whose calm, methodical demeanor contrasted with his own driven nature. The cyclotron team introduced a number of improvements to the system, particularly through the development of high-charge, high-intensity heavy-ion sources, which significantly expanded the mass and energy ranges of the accelerated particles.[11]

The CRC was an interfaculty, international, and interdisciplinary platform. Its board of directors included physicists, chemists, physicians, and engineers. The scientific council comprised professors from five major Belgian universities. It welcomed international collaborations across Europe and beyond.[12] Its culture was highly open and collaborative, shaping IBA's philosophy. CYCLONE's beam time was shared among disciplines such as physics, chemistry, and applied sciences. Beyond fundamental research, the center began producing radioisotopes for nuclear medicine, like radioactive iodine 123, used to diagnose thyroid disorders. Professor André Wambersie, head of radiotherapy at the UCL clinics, proposed using the cyclotron to treat cancerous tumors with high-energy neutron beams, thereby making the Louvain-la-Neuve cyclotron one of the few laboratories in the world where neutron therapy would be developed from 1978 onwards.

The CRC's openness to the world of applications and industry allowed Yves' team to gain a clear understanding of the importance of user experience and the customer's perspective, essential factors in the company's later successful growth. Yves had been immersed in this vibrant techno-scientific and human environment for fourteen years when he took a sabbatical year at Berkeley. This temporary break prompted him to reevaluate the impact that cyclotrons could have on society.

From fundamental to medical

Standing on his balcony overlooking San Francisco Bay, Yves developed the idea that the cyclotron of the future could be widely used for industrial or medical applications, such as the production of radioisotopes on a far larger scale. However, the machines of the time were not suited to mass distribution. Each had a unique design, and energy efficiency was not considered at all. Substantial progress could be made in energy consumption, reliability, robustness, and ease of use by less specialized personnel.

The seed was sown. In parallel with his work on developing the new 88 inch cyclotron source in Berkeley, Yves began to imagine what an ideal industrial cyclotron might be: how might the electromagnet be better designed? How could the accelerating structure be removed from the magnet's air gap in order to reduce the required power? These fundamental questions would form the basis for the design of all IBA cyclotrons thereafter. To test his ideas, Yves presented a preliminary design for a 40 MeV separated sector cyclotron with reduced energy consumption at the Tenth International Conference on Cyclotrons and Their Applications, held in May 1984 at Michigan State University.

When he returned to Louvain-la-Neuve in July, there was no shortage of projects. The lessons learned in Berkeley needed to be transposed to the CRC, where a new "Octopus" ion source for physics research was being built, using an 8 pole magnet. But another event accelerated the timeline: during Yves's absence, the university had purchased a positron camera, which had recently been installed near the cyclotron. The cyclotron was producing radioisotopes every morning for medical research in positron emission tomography (PET), an emerging medical imaging method that enables 3D, real-time visualization of the human body's metabolism.

To decongest the cyclotron, physicists considered constructing a "small" additional accelerator dedicated to medical research. Yves saw this as the perfect opportunity to develop the machine he had begun to envision in California, rather than merely copying existing models. On average, two or three cyclotrons were sold each year worldwide for the industrial production of radioisotopes. Although only about twenty were then operational, these smaller cyclotrons offered a promising alternative to the traditional method of producing radioisotopes with nuclear reactors.

Without seeking approval or a mandate, Yves began designing a new cyclotron capable of accelerating protons between 15 and 30 MeV. He consistently kept in mind the needs of radioisotope producers, who were frustrated by the complexity and low efficiency of existing devices. His clear goal was to produce a beam far more intense than existing machines, improve energy efficiency, make control easier—ideally automatic—and simplify maintenance. Above all, he envisioned an extraction system that eliminated excessive losses: no more fragile electrostatic deflectors that melted when the current exceeded a given threshold. This drove him to explore a bold new approach: instead of accelerating protons, he would accelerate negative hydrogen ions (H^-) and "strip" them using a thin sheet of carbon at extraction.

The idea was not new, but the few companies attempting to commercialize it had failed. Such was the case of the American firm, The Cyclotron Corporation (TCC), founded by Ernest Lawrence's godson, which had gone bankrupt shortly after launching its CP42 model. Yves believed this failure stemmed from the ion source positioned at the center of the machine, which polluted the vacuum. His innovative solution was to place the source outside the cyclotron and inject the beam into the spiral using an axial injection system, a method he had already tested in his research on heavy-ion acceleration for experimental physics.

For weeks, Yves refined these concepts before consulting his colleague, Gérard Lannoye, at the CRC design office. Together, they sketched plans for a circular magnet—more efficient for magnetism and cheaper to manufacture—and outlined the overall architecture of the new cyclotron. In the winter of 1985, Yves traveled to the Grand Accélérateur National d'Ions Lourds (Large Heavy Ion National Accelerator: GANIL) in Caen to perform magnetic field calculations using software unavailable in Louvain-la-Neuve. When he returned, he estimated the parameters of the accelerating cavities, corrected the remaining approximations with a scale model, and completed the design.

The result was the promise of an extraordinary cyclotron: the future Cyclone 30—five times more powerful, three times more energy efficient, and far easier to maintain than its competitors. A robust, automated accelerator engineered for the mass production of radioisotopes, capable of securing IBA a singular position in the global market. A prototype would still be needed to prove its worth, but on paper, this machine already represented a quiet revolution.

From concept to business

Designing the prototype for the new cyclotron raised an important question: how could it be financed? The first step was to turn to the CRC's usual channels, especially the Interuniversity Institute for Nuclear Sciences (IISN). However, the proposed machine, designed for industrial use, fell outside the usual scope of academic research. For that reason, Pierre Macq encouraged Yves to meet with Claire Demain, head of UCL's research–industry liaison unit. Interested in the project, she played a key role on several levels. First, she stressed the importance of filing for a patent immediately, since Yves planned to present his new concept at Vancouver's renowned International Particle Accelerator Conference, and unveiling the innovation without protection was out of the question. Next, she approached Belgian industrial players who might be interested in joining the venture. Her efforts led nowhere: neither Belgonucléaire nor ACEC showed interest. She then mobilized her political network to secure funding, notably through Melchior Wathelet (Senior), the Walloon Minister for SMEs and New Technologies. He agreed to support the prototype on one condition: the Walloon Region would finance 75 percent of the project, provided that a company was established to develop and commercialize it, contributing to the region's economy. The combined involvement of regional public authorities and university leadership proved decisive at this stage and remained vital throughout the company's early development.

Yves quickly embraced the idea of leaving the security of academia to pursue an entrepreneurial journey—especially because he envisioned a company built on social purpose and collaboration. Encouraged by Claire Demain and Pierre Macq, he set out to improve his management skills by taking evening classes at the Institut d'Administration et de Gestion (IAG) and, with guidance from one of his professors, drafted a financial plan for the future company. His goal? A small, nimble team of about fifteen people, generating profit through the sale of one cyclotron annually, supported by services and spare parts—with an estimated annual turnover of 100 million Belgian francs (€2.5 million).

The second challenge in establishing the company was raising the start-up capital. Building the cyclotron prototype would cost 60 million Belgian francs (€1.5 million). The Walloon Region had committed to covering 75 percent of that amount in the form of a recoverable advance, leaving 15 million to be raised as equity capital, plus an additional 10 million to cover expenses before the first revenues arrived—a total of 25 million francs (€625,000).

An initial tranche of 8 million francs (€200,000) was secured from the CRC, generated from services provided to external clients. The agreement was quite complex, as this fundraising came shortly after the bankruptcy of UCL's first spin-off, Acade, which had caused university officials to be cautious about engaging in such ventures again.

The team then approached René Constant, the General Manager and founder of the Institut National des Radioéléments (IRE). The IRE was a natural partner, as it had already used the UCL cyclotron to produce radioisotopes. It invested 12 million francs (€300,000). Initially, the remaining funds were to be covered by a one-million-franc (€25,000) loan from Yves Jongen and a four-million-franc (€100,000) contribution from his father, Robert; these contributions would have completed the necessary capital to start the company.

With the financing in place, the next step was to formalize agreements among the shareholders. To do this, Claire Demain hired a talented young attorney, Olivier Ralet, who would become a trusted legal advisor and a member of IBA's board of directors.

First IBA logo, depicting the axial injection system used to send the beam into the cyclotron spiral from an external source, 1986.

The negotiations proved complex. The university, represented by Claire Demain, asked for 10 million founders' shares and royalties in exchange for a license to the cyclotron patent. Pierre Macq wanted the prototype to stay at UCL, but a compromise was reached: the new company would keep ownership of the machine while giving the university free use. At the same time, support from the nuclear physicists was secured, despite initial resistance from a few who saw the monetization of fundamental research results as a form of "prostitution." In the end, most saw the project as an opportunity—especially in a regional context marked by economic crisis, record unemployment, and shrinking research budgets.

The company name *Ion Beam Applications* was chosen for its worldwide presence and its clear emphasis on applications rather than fundamental research.

Just as everything was in place for the official founding of IBA at the end of March 1986, an unexpected obstacle emerged. Jean Hallet, the somewhat conservative chairman of UCL's board of directors, opposed Yves Jongen and his father's personal investment in the company's capital. In Hallet's view, such participation blurred the line between capital and labor. Forced to comply with this last-minute demand, the university—somewhat embarrassed—found a solution at the last minute: its holding company Transec (later Sopartec), controlled by UCL and led by André Rostenne, agreed to contribute the missing five million francs. IBA was officially founded on March 28, 1986.

The winds of change: the Cyclone 30

Throwing caution to the wind, Yves Jongen—driven by a desire to commercialize his innovation as quickly as possible—began constructing the Cyclone 30 prototype in September 1985, even before the company was officially established. This initial phase was funded with CRC resources allocated for IBA's future investment. Subcontractors from the regional industrial network were mobilized: FAFER in Charleroi supplied high-quality magnetic steel plates; ACEC manufactured the magnet; Sigmaphi in Brittany produced the coils; and Brussels-based Jema provided the power supply. The magnet, the component with the longest lead time, was ordered first.

By the time IBA was founded in March 1986, the magnet was already nearing completion. In early May, its components were delivered to the CRC, where IBA rented space for assembly. At that point, Yves was the company's only employee, working part-time. He hired two electricians and two mechanics through a temporary work agency and brought them on as full-time staff that November. He insisted on granting every team member employee status, refusing the idea of hourly workers and time clocks, and instead advocating for individual responsibility in every role.

The magnet assembly started in May 1986. The precision needed for the magnetic field was extremely high—down to a few hundredths of a millimeter. Unlike standard practices of the time, which used corrective coils, Yves took an innovative approach: adjusting the field once and for all at the factory by iteratively refining the magnet's pole profile. This method ensured very low power consumption of just 7 kW, compared to about 100 kW for similar machines. The first magnetic field map, completed in June, was a complete failure. The three-dimensional magnet had been modeled on a two-dimensional computer program. In contrast to his usual openness, Yves did not show his disappointment; he wanted to avoid discouraging the team. He quickly designed iron blocks to reinforce the field where needed. After several iterations and two months of intense work, the magnetic field finally met the required specifications.

Meanwhile, the development of the external ion source faced its own challenges. The originally planned ECR technique proved ineffective for producing negative ions. A new method was adopted: the *Multicusp* ion source, which generated a high-intensity ion beam by creating a dense, stable plasma.

The study of the radiofrequency system—responsible for accelerating ions through the electrodes (the "Dees")—was carried out by CRC engineer Jean-Louis Bol and Yves Jongen. Thanks to its meticulous design, this highly innovative system required only 10 kW of power, compared to the usual 50 to 70 kW. However, the mechanically welded aluminum vacuum chamber proved porous once built. After several unsuccessful attempts to re-weld it, an epoxy varnish was applied to seal the chamber, causing a one-month delay.

Once the magnetic field was calibrated, the vacuum chamber and radiofrequency components were assembled in October. After a few days spent sealing minor leaks, the vacuum was satisfactory. Testing of the radiofrequency system began, but an electrical discharge caused a short circuit in the aluminum electrodes. Recognizing that aluminum was a poor choice of material, the team quickly crafted new copper electrodes and replaced the Dee supports with solid copper. After a few days of conditioning, the required voltage was successfully achieved.

By mid-November, the cyclotron was nearly finished. Temporary shielding made of concrete blocks was erected around the machine for the initial tests. These first trials were limited to low intensities because the shielding did not cover the entire device.

On December 23, after a full day of adjustments, the first injection was performed. Despite an initially low yield, by 2:00 a.m. on December 24, the first beam reached the cyclotron's maximum energy. It was a resounding success—achieved just nine months after IBA's founding. The team had worked tirelessly around the clock to overcome obstacles and unforeseen complications. It was time to pop open the champagne.

After a short holiday break, the beam extraction devices were installed in January 1987. In early February, the first beam was extracted with 100 percent efficiency. However, the maximum intensity could not be tested due to insufficient shielding. Meanwhile, construction began on a new building with three-meter-thick walls, designed by Marc Lejeune of the Faculty of Applied Sciences, to house the cyclotron. The final calculations for the central geometry were incorporated during this period, enhancing overall performance.

In June, the cyclotron was relocated and reassembled in its new facility. Two months of intensive tuning enabled the prototype to meet all its specifications: up to 500 μA of extracted beam at peak performance—five times the capacity of any existing radioisotope production cyclotron—while maintaining electrical consumption at just 90 kW. The prototype proved to be a complete success, ready to be delivered to industrial radioisotope producers worldwide.

Yves Jongen setting up the first Cyclone 30
at the CRC, circa 1986-1987.

A ROCKY START

[1988-1997]

2

One of the rare shipments of a Cyclone 30 by plane. This one was headed to the National Medical Cyclotron Centre in Sydney, Australia, circa 1990.

argo
IBA
Ion Beam Applications
FAG KZF 0034
Franke

The world or nothing

The young team at IBA had achieved a remarkable technical feat by developing, almost without a hitch, its first internally developed industrial cyclotron optimized for radioisotope production. The next challenge was to promote and to sell it. The market was small, highly specialized, and global. Shareholders were cautious about a young academic team's ability to take on established industry players. The original recommendation was to partner with an experienced manufacturer, such as the French firm CGR-MeV, a subsidiary of Thomson CSF; the Swedish firm Scanditronix; or the Japanese firm Sumitomo. The first contacts proved difficult. Proud of their own machines, the competitors struggled to believe that a Belgian university team could have designed a cyclotron that was five times more powerful, three times more energy-efficient, and fully automated. Negotiations with CGR-Mev quickly broke down, as the company had already decided—without revealing it—to withdraw from the market. Discussions with Scanditronix and Sumitomo continued slowly. Even after a successful demonstration of the prototype, Scanditronix engineers remained skeptical, considering the design too disruptive. This refusal, initially met with bitter disappointment, turned out to be a blessing in disguise. It allowed IBA to survive, retain its full margin, and remain viable in the long term.

By early 1987, the lack of industrial partners made creating a sales function essential. Yves Jongen aimed to recruit a talented salesperson—if not yet highly experienced—because he doubted that the salary he could offer for such a role in an unknown startup would attract a seasoned pro. He asked professors for recommendations, including Philippe de Woot of the IAG, requesting them to identify the most promising recent graduates. Two names kept coming up: Pierre Mottet and Serge Lamisse. Pierre Mottet, who was working at IBM at the time, was the first to agree to meet. He sat down with Yves at the Café des Halles in Louvain-la-Neuve. After several evenings of lively discussion, he was convinced by the project's boldness. On Easter Monday 1987, he decided to join IBA, leaving a promising corporate career to take a chance on the startup

—much like Yves did when he left academia to pursue entrepreneurship. One letter changed everything: from IBM to IBA, his destiny was shifted. His first office—a quickly converted coffee room in a grim UCL building—hardly provided ideal conditions for welcoming clients and prospects. Serge Lamisse joined IBA a few months later.

The year 1987 marked the takeoff of IBA's commercial activities. After several relatively quiet years, the cyclotron market showed clear signs of recovery. Projects began to emerge at universities in Germany, Australia, Iran, China, and Belgium. While awaiting Pierre Mottet's formal appointment, Yves took the initiative. He contacted the manager of the Australian project, who was wary of negative-ion cyclotron technology in the wake of the bankruptcy of TCC, a company that had previously attempted to commercialize this approach. Undeterred, Yves succeeded in persuading him to allow a presentation of the innovation to senior physicists at the Australian Nuclear Science and Technology Organisation (ANSTO) in Sydney. The presentation made a strong impression. The next stop was Canberra, where Yves met with the Belgian ambassador, who provided valuable backing for a project considered strategic by the Australian government.

Back in Belgium, Yves and Pierre drafted a comprehensive business plan. IBA made its first public appearances at industry conferences, especially in Nice and Toronto. Despite a modest 10-square-meter booth—and a suit hastily purchased to replace the one Yves lost with his luggage at the airport—they made many new contacts, including Medi+Physics, the American leader in radioisotope production and a subsidiary of the Swiss group Hoffmann-La Roche. Pierre, who had become a cyclotron expert through pure determination, immediately started a tour of North American cyclotron sites to pitch the concept. This was followed by IBA's participation in the European Conference on Nuclear Medicine in Budapest.

By the end of summer, Pierre had identified about a dozen prospects, including Medi+Physics, as well as Canadian and Chinese projects, along with ongoing European and Australian initiatives. The first opportunity to materialize was with Medi+Physics. In October, two of its executives visited Louvain-la-Neuve. One of them, a veteran engineer, was immediately convinced by the Cyclone 30's ease of use and power. During the visit, a technical issue caused by a failing transformer was expertly managed by an IBA team familiar with the problem. While engineers worked to fix it during lunch, Yves and Pierre deliberately extended the meal, ensuring the issue was fully resolved before the visitors returned. The delegates left convinced and ready to recommend purchasing IBA's cyclotron. A letter of intent was signed at Christmas. Meanwhile, however, the dollar had declined. The first of many dilemmas emerged: sell without a profit margin or risk not selling at all? And on which specifications—maximum performance at 500 µA, or the safer option of 350 µA? Pierre and Yves started learning how to face and balance their different views on risk.

Contract negotiations with Medi+Physics continued and culminated in February 1988 in New York. IBA managed to secure a support letter from its shareholders—the university and the IRE—in place of bank guarantees it couldn't obtain. To influence the outcome, Yves agreed to be available to the client to complete the project if any difficulties arose. Due to an unexpected timing coincidence with Valentine's Day—prompting the American negotiators to finish discussions sooner—it also helped the agreement succeed. After this initial sale, earlier cyclotron designs became obsolete.

Other opportunities quickly arose. A contract to transfer the Cyclone 30 design to China, including key component supplies, was signed with a Beijing-based customer. This strategic move involved significant intellectual property risks, but it was essential to secure cash flow. In hindsight, the decision proved wise: no local competitor would be able to master the technology for many years. Subsequent orders from China continued to be placed directly with IBA in Belgium. This agreement helped IBA establish a presence in emerging markets. The local representative, Frank Uytterhaegen, played a crucial role in the company's success in the rapidly expanding Chinese market. A well-known collector of modern Chinese art and a close associate of artist Ai Weiwei, Uytterhaegen repeatedly proved invaluable within Belgian diplomatic circles.

In Japan's highly protectionist market, the competitor Sumitomo turned to IBA to supply a high-performance ion source for the large research cyclotron at the Japan Atomic Energy Research Institute (JAERI). The agreement resulted in a contract worth 44 million Belgian francs (€1.1 million), signed in March 1988. Around the same time, the Australian contract was finalized. Two years later, Nihon Medi-Physics—a joint venture between Hoffmann-La Roche and Sumitomo—purchased a new cyclotron in Japan, choosing IBA's machine over Sumitomo's own in-house model.

Meanwhile, the sales team grew with the addition of Sybille van den Hove, Ahmet Cokragan, and Sabine de Voghel—three young graduates whose enthusiasm and dedication helped propel the company's early commercial success. IBA quickly positioned itself as an international player capable of reaching even the most remote markets, a feat that demanded complete flexibility from both the sales and installation teams. Ironically, Yves himself suffered from air sickness—a condition he eased by focusing on calculations and sketches for new machines during flights. This habit led Pierre to joke, with amusement: "Preventing him from traveling was the surest way to control the R&D budget."

Frank Uyterhaegen (third from left), Pierre Mottet (center), and Yves Jongen (second from right) visiting China to finalize a technology transfer agreement, 1987.

Physicist Claude Dupont installing IBA's Octopus source at Japan's JAERI center, 1988.

In Belgium, the Université Libre de Bruxelles' (ULB) Erasmus Hospital announced its plan to acquire a small PET cyclotron. IBA proposed its 30 MeV model—more powerful than the rival offer from the American firm CTI—at a competitive price. However, the hospital also required automated targets and chemistry systems, an area where IBA had no prior experience. Confronted with American dominance in this field, IBA embarked on an ambitious, fast-track development program. Within just six months, the company had to design, manufacture, and demonstrate high-performance positron targets as well as automated chemistry systems. To meet this challenge, it relied on the expertise of the UCL positron camera team, particularly that of a young engineer, Jean-Luc Morelle. Once again, the young company demonstrated remarkable speed and execution, securing the contract through close collaboration with the university.

By the end of 1987, the principle of employee and director share ownership was officially established through a capital increase available to all employees on the same terms as the founders. Staff participation rose to 25 percent of the capital, alongside 35 percent for the IRE, 24 percent for UCL, and 15 percent for Transec.

The fine art of juggling with risk

Between 1988 and 1991, IBA experienced rapid growth driven by the commercial success of the Cyclone 30. Although the initial goal was to sell one cyclotron each year, five contracts were signed in 1988 alone. Each sale was celebrated with high spirits and popping corks. The IBA startup succeeded where many others had failed: it brought to market a product precisely aligned with customer needs, sold through a global search for prospects and a sales force that was remarkably effective for such a small team. This unexpected success fueled ongoing expansion. In three years, the company grew from 11 to 139 employees, in an atmosphere of enthusiasm, improvisation, and solidarity. The momentum quickly made the first relocation inevitable. The team moved from the austere corridors of the physics department to hastily built prefabricated buildings set up in a parking lot—an interim solution while waiting for more permanent facilities.

Most importantly, IBA quickly learned to manage the peaks and valleys in demand typical of this niche market. Industrialization soon became a major challenge. Under Jean-Louis Bol's leadership, it was built around three guiding principles—quality, lead time, and cost—with customer satisfaction firmly at the heart of the process. To deliver these complex machines on time, IBA adopted a set of simple yet radical decisions. The company outsourced the manufacturing of all components while keeping responsibility for design, engineering, and final assembly. An assembly hall in Andenne was leased from Pégard, a manufacturer of large metal parts. High-precision power supplies were sourced from Jema, which derived a significant portion of its revenue from IBA and would later turn to the company for support when facing the risk of bankruptcy. In this way, a dense, local, industrial ecosystem formed, fulfilling the original promise of economic benefits for the region.

Internally, the company culture was open and transparent, based on teamwork, technical excellence, strong commercial involvement, and the simple joy of working together. Philippe de Woot, who took on the role of chairman of IBA's board of directors for an initial term of just six months, became deeply involved in the company's development. He generously shared his experience, developed a keen interest in the spin-off, and used it as a case study for future generations of UCL students. He held his position until 2004, leaving a lasting impact on the company through his humanistic, values-driven approach to governance.

Determined to maintain its momentum and guard against potential market downturns, IBA looked ahead by developing even smaller and more affordable cyclotrons designed to be installed directly in hospitals for the purpose of producing PET radioisotopes. These substances, which have very short half-lives—ranging from minutes to hours—must be produced as close as possible to the examination site.

Recognizing the potential of this emerging market, even though it was already served by established players—some of which marketed both accelerators and PET cameras—IBA initiated strategic discussions with General Electric, Positron Corporation, Siemens-CTI, and venture-capital firms to create a U.S. subsidiary and develop a so-called "baby cyclotron." The anticipated funding failed to materialize. Nevertheless, the team proceeded with the design of the Cyclone 10/5, using deposits paid on Cyclone 30 orders to finance the effort. This was followed by the Cyclone 18/9 and the Cyclone 3D, the world's smallest medical cyclotron. In parallel, target-production and chemistry modules were developed for Erasmus Hospital, including fluorodeoxyglucose (FDG)—the main radioactive tracer used to assess tissue metabolic activity and diagnose various diseases, including cancer.

To avoid isolation among industry giants, in 1990, IBA entered into a collaboration agreement with CPS, a joint venture between Siemens and CTI, which then held the majority of the global PET market. IBA aimed to leverage its partner's sales network and offered an exclusive license for its baby cyclotrons.

Newsletter announcing the development of TEP radioisotope production systems, Cyclone 10/5 and 3D, 1988.

The IBA team welcoming its Japanese partners from Sumitomo in the prefabricated offices erected in the UCL car park, April 1989.

The Cyclone 18/9 later became a bestseller in the world of radiopharmacy. The designer of the advert hired a tall model to highlight the machine's compactness.

In addition to its own model, CPS started offering two IBA cyclotron models to its hospital customers. In the United States, the small sales team assembled by Serge Lamisse proved it could compete on equal footing with the Siemens-CTI team. Since it did not yet have a commercial hospital cyclotron to showcase, the team relied on the proven robustness of the Cyclone 30 and adopted a successful strategy of moving down-market to "evangelize potential customers".

The agreement with Siemens greatly boosted IBA's credibility and drew the interest of top venture capital investors, led by Philippe Janssens of Euroventures, who bought a 36 percent stake in the company. His ongoing support was crucial to financing the multiple product lines on which IBA's future depended.

Representing UCL on IBA's board of directors, Professor Jean Vervier expressed a concern that captured the moment: "Are Yves Jongen and his team taking on too many projects, risking dispersion and neglecting current production, which is already a significant challenge?"[13] In fact, this dynamic proved vital to IBA's survival during its early years.

Other avenues of diversification were explored simultaneously. IBA researched ion implantation technologies for semiconductors, microfiltration membranes for microbiology, a method for measuring metal component wear through irradiation in Canada, and an industrial imaging project for the Channel Tunnel. Most of these initiatives were either discontinued or pursued outside of IBA.[14] In contrast, in 1990, proton therapy became part of the company's strategic horizon, followed in 1991 by the Rhodotron—an electron accelerator that would soon command headlines.

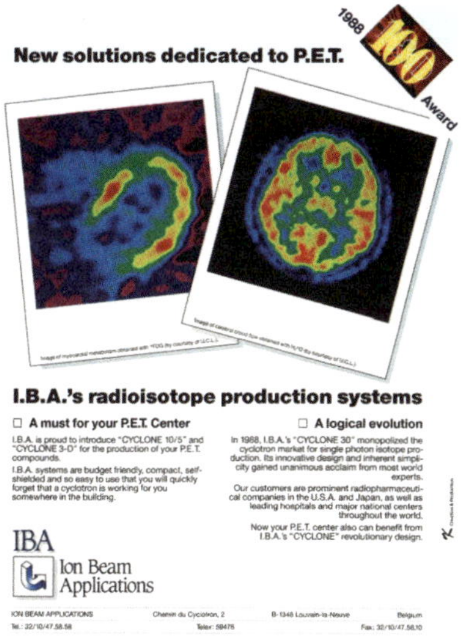

New solutions dedicated to P.E.T.

1988 100 Award

I.B.A.'s radioisotope production systems

☐ A must for your P.E.T. Center

I.B.A. is proud to introduce "CYCLONE 10/5" and "CYCLONE 3-D" for the production of your P.E.T. compounds.

I.B.A. systems are budget friendly, compact, self-shielded and so easy to use that you will quickly forget that a cyclotron is working for you somewhere in the building.

☐ A logical evolution

In 1988, I.B.A.'s "CYCLONE 30" monopolized the cyclotron market for single photon isotope production. Its innovative design and inherent simplicity gained unanimous acclaim from most world experts.

Our customers are prominent radiopharmaceutical companies in the U.S.A. and Japan, as well as leading hospitals and major national centers throughout the world.

Now your P.E.T. center also can benefit from I.B.A.'s "CYCLONE" revolutionary design.

IBA
Ion Beam Applications

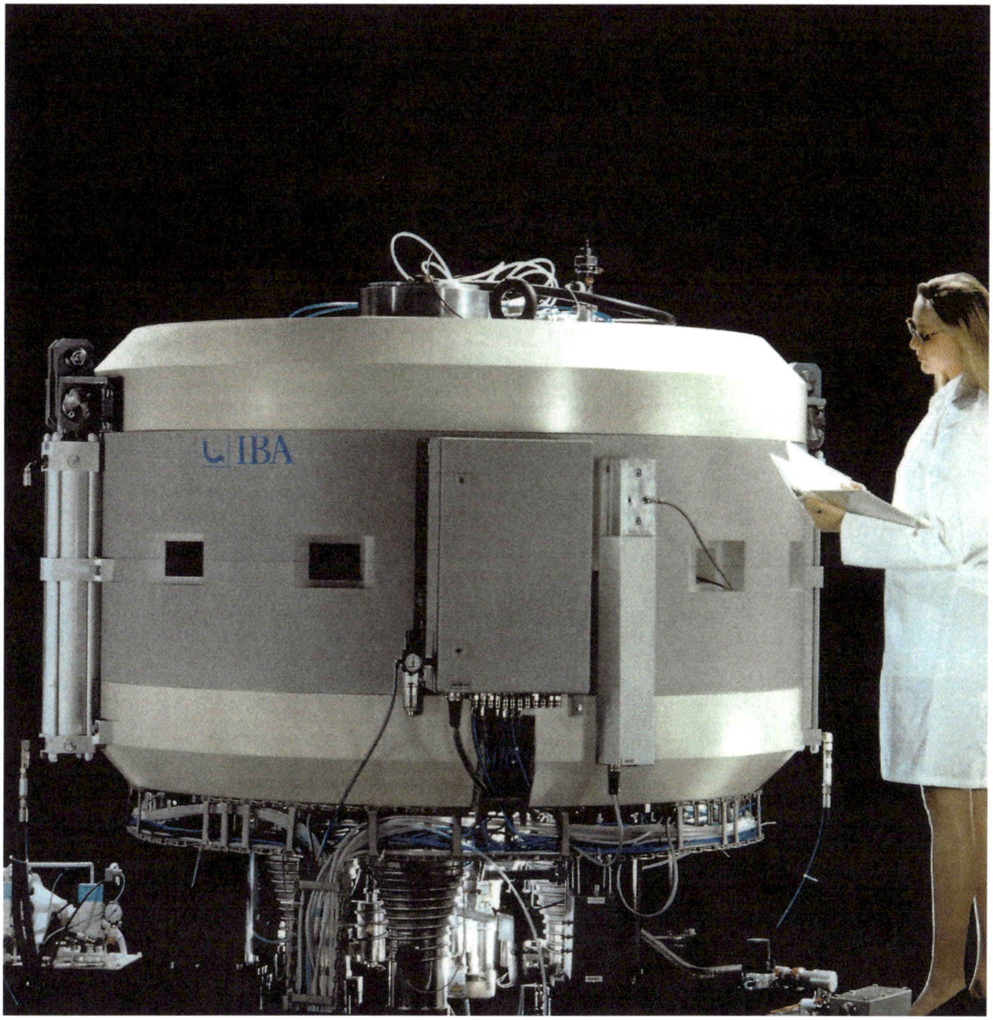

ION BEAM APPLICATIONS Chemin du Cyclotron, 2 B-1348 Louvain-la-Neuve Belgium
Tel.: 32/10/47.58.58 Telex: 59475 Fax: 32/10/47.58.10

The big leap toward proton therapy

Toward the end of 1989, at the height of this creative whirlwind, Yves Jongen received a call from Professor André Wambersie, director of radiotherapy at UCL. Both men understood that "every time a physicist accelerates a new type of beam, physicians wonder what they can do with it".[15]

André Wambersie, who was always seeking advances in nuclear medicine, had heard about an experimental project at a small university in Loma Linda, California. Using a synchrotron built by Fermi National Accelerator Laboratory near Chicago, Loma Linda University Medical Center (LLUMC) was preparing to treat its first patient with proton therapy. Wambersie had previously experimented with this emerging approach, originally developed at Harvard University based on William Bragg's discovery and early trials in Berkeley and Uppsala in the 1950s. The technique now seemed ready for hospital-based clinical use. Thanks to strong political support, Loma Linda outpaced the more prestigious Massachusetts General Hospital (MGH) in Boston. Professor Wambersie asked Yves if he could design a cyclotron that would be simpler and less expensive than the Loma Linda synchrotron, which had cost $60 million.

Neutron therapy, previously tested under Wambersie's leadership, revealed its limitations: the ballistic properties of neutrons were not suitable for replacing conventional radiotherapy. Proton therapy, on the other hand, offered the ability to target tumors with great precision while protecting surrounding healthy tissue, thus reducing side effects. A market study conducted by an external consultant indicated significant potential, estimating that up to twenty centers could be established worldwide within five years. Yves immediately embraced the idea. During a long flight, he sketched an outline of a 230 MeV cyclotron designed to reach tumors up to 32 centimeters deep in the body, following the well-known Bragg peak, where positively charged particles deliver their maximum radiation dose at a specific depth before stopping abruptly. This vision entailed designing a 200-ton accelerator and a whole supporting system—including rotating treatment gantries as large as a three-story building, silently circling a patient and capable of directing a proton beam into tissue with millimeter accuracy. IBA was preparing to progress from diagnosis to cancer treatment.

The strategy was crystal clear: "Proton therapy only has a future if the equipment and its management can be made affordable".[16] Synergies with existing activities were advantageous. Part of the R&D program would be funded by the sale of the prototype and the initial systems, and partly by the Walloon Region as a recoverable advance, similar to what had been done with Cyclone 30 and most other research programs. To lower the risk for a small or medium-sized enterprise, IBA formed a partnership with Sumitomo. Development responsibilities were shared equally; Sumitomo promoted the products in Asia and the Middle East, while IBA handled the rest of the world. The first potential client appeared in Antwerp: Middelheim Hospital, where Professor Pierre Scalliet worked. However, due to the complexity of the Belgian institutional landscape, it would take nearly thirty years for IBA to gain recognition in its own country. The major opportunity, however, came from the United States. In late 1992, Massachusetts General Hospital issued a call for tenders for a system with a $20 million budget, funded by a grant from the National Cancer Institute (NCI).

This contract was more than just a business deal for IBA: it could potentially open the door to global recognition, technical and scientific credibility, and, most importantly, direct access to the heart of proton therapy training ecosystem. Facing giants such as Siemens, Varian, Westinghouse, and General Atomics, the modest Belgian company appeared out of its league—a bit like "a parish team in a Division One championship".[17] To meet the NCI's requirements,

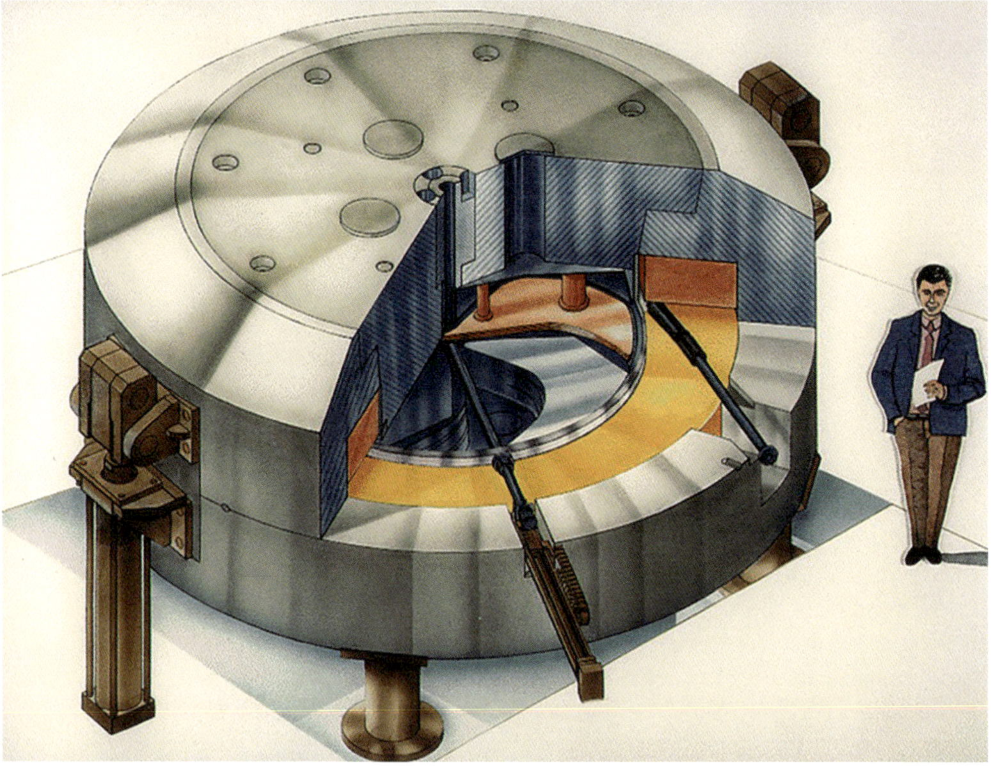

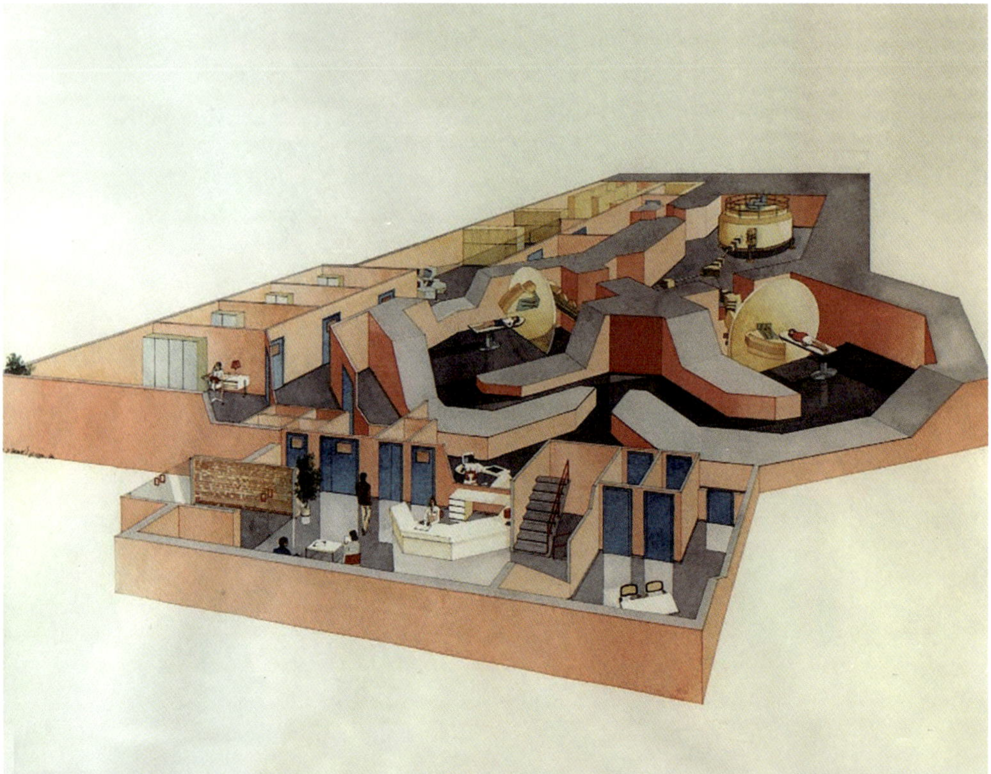

Preliminary drawings of the Cyclone 230 and a two-room proton therapy center designed for the hospital in Antwerp, circa 1991.

IBA had to secure a $20 million bank guarantee. However, its main banker, Générale de Banque, refused. Undeterred, IBA decided to participate in the project as a subcontractor to General Atomics. But in a dramatic turn of events, just two months before the deadline, General Atomics withdrew, citing legal risks specific to the United States. A response was organized in record time. Thanks to the decisive role of Yves Windelinckx, head of the Office National du Ducroire (ONDD), the Belgian export agency, IBA secured a banking pool led by Banque Bruxelles Lambert. Générale de Banque joined at the last minute, contingent upon the obligation of an emergency capital increase. This increase was underwritten by the Walloon Regional Investment Company (SRIW), subject to strict conditions that were highly dilutive to shareholders. Behind the scenes, a frantic race against time began, fraught with disagreements and sleepless nights spent printing thousands of pages of the bid. The proposal was submitted in May 1993. Against all odds, IBA won the bid. It was the only company willing to fully embrace the project and accept the specifications. One of the experts on the American award committee quipped: "This contract will probably spell the end for several accelerator companies around the world—perhaps those that don't get the contract, but certainly the one that does!" He was not entirely wrong—except for IBA, which managed to survive the unexpected twists and turns of this unprecedented project. The contract was signed in April 1994. More than just a technical and commercial triumph, it was a landmark achievement that positioned IBA as an emerging global leader.

The rose and the electron

Not satisfied with pursuing multiple development paths, IBA identified another major industrial opportunity in the early 1990s: electron accelerator applications for sterilization and polymer crosslinking. However, its ambitions were initially limited by a lack of expertise in linear accelerators (Linac), which were dominant in the market at the time. The turning point occurred when the French Atomic Energy Commission (CEA) invited IBA executives to Orsay to see a prototype accelerator called Rhodotron, named because the particles followed a path shaped like rose petals. This device had been developed in relative secrecy by engineer Jacques Pottier, without a specific mandate from the CEA, as it was not part of their core business. For the experts at IBA, it was love at first sight. Yves immediately recognized the enormous potential of this innovative concept, which combined existing technologies to deliver exceptional performance. The Rhodotron could operate at energies of 5 to 10 MeV and power outputs exceeding 100 kW, while offering improved reliability, safety, and continuous operation. Unlike traditional Linac, it was technologically similar to a cyclotron, making it a natural fit for IBA's expertise. In particular, IBA's advanced knowledge in high-frequency engineering, developed through cyclotron research led by outstanding engineers such as Michel Abs, would enable the prototype to be refined and scaled up for industrial production.

On December 12, 1991, an exclusive licensing agreement was signed, which transferred all technology rights to IBA in exchange for royalties on future sales. Production would stay in France or Belgium. This agreement earned the CEA's award for best technology transfer in 1995.

In commercial terms, the Rhodotron mainly targeted the medical sterilization market, while also offering strong opportunities in polymerization, water treatment, food pasteurization, and industrial waste recovery. The Rhodotron was more than just a product—it represented a disruptive strategy, opening up a new promising market for IBA that had previously been mainly controlled by Sumitomo and MDS Nordion. Thanks to its technical performance, versatility across different industrial sectors, and a solid scientific partnership, the Rhodotron was positioned to become a new technological pillar of IBA's growth in the coming decades. However, its industrialization took nearly two years, and its commercial launch was slower than expected. The first customer was the Swiss firm Stüder, a European leader in cable irradiation and a loyal IBA customer ever since.

IBA
An IBA / CEA Collaboration

The first Rhodotron TT300 installed at Stüder AG in Switzerland for the irradiation of polymer cables, 1996.

From creativity to profitability

In 1991, IBA moved from its prefabricated buildings to a new facility that included offices and an assembly hall, located just a stone's throw from Rue Lenoir. The company had found a permanent home. Thanks to the ingenuity of its exceptional team of engineers and technicians, IBA laid the groundwork for future success by diversifying risks and opportunities across five distinct product lines in three markets: medical imaging, cancer therapy, and industrial ionization.

The therapeutic branch was further expanded with the addition of brachytherapy. In 1992, IBA's success with PET cyclotrons caught the attention of Theragenics, a Georgia Tech spin-off based in Atlanta specializing in radiological equipment. This company focused on a new method for treating prostate cancer using brachytherapy, which involved implanting tiny capsules containing palladium-103 into the tumor. Until then, this radioisotope was produced from palladium-102, an extremely rare natural isotope, enriched by an electromagnetic separator and then irradiated in the Oak Ridge nuclear reactor. John Carden, president of Theragenics, first approached IBA requesting an electromagnetic separator to process palladium-102, as the supply from Oak Ridge was nearly exhausted. Although this request was within IBA's capabilities, Yves responded that a theoretical alternative had been demonstrated by bombarding rhodium with an accelerator. However, Carden argued that leading experts had concluded it was impossible to design a cyclotron capable of generating enough beam intensity at a reasonable cost. For IBA, this meant developing a beam three times as powerful as the Cyclone 30. Yves asked Serge Lamisse, who had introduced Theragenics to Louvain-la-Neuve, to take the delegation out for lunch. During the break, Yves gathered his team of experts and asked if they were prepared to design a brand-new cyclotron model based on the Cyclone 18/9, with a multiplied beam—even if it meant working around the clock. When they returned from lunch, Yves told Theragenics they could build it in eighteen months. Carden accepted and proposed an extra $1 million bonus if the device was delivered within twelve months. The team achieved another miracle: 360 days later, the 18+ cyclotron produced its first beam in Atlanta. Yves described the scope of the task to the Belgian press: "It's as if we had produced a car engine powerful enough to propel a thirty-ton truck or a large barge".[18] This kind of achievement led to an internal maxim: "We didn't know it was impossible, so we did it! And several times a day!"

Despite this latest technical and commercial achievement, the company's rapid growth—driven by specific customer needs—had not yet generated substantial profits. One recurring challenge was the unpredictability of cyclotron order cycles. "We are able to compete successfully, but we have no influence over when the customer places an order", management explained to its board of directors.[19] This would become a constant theme in IBA's history, one that successive management teams would have to work around.

Baby cyclotrons, for example, did not sell as well as anticipated. The segment proved fiercely competitive, and reimbursement from the U.S. Social Security system was slow to materialize. What's more, the collaboration with CPS failed to yield the expected results, as the partner tended to sell its own devices to customers. Eventually, IBA took costly legal action to terminate the collaboration and regain its freedom of action.

Between 1989 and 1994, the company suffered a series of financial losses. To prepare for the future, it invested larger sums in its development than its operations could cover, making up the difference through repeated capital

Offices and assembly hall
on Rue Lenoir, 1991. IBA is here to stay.

The IBA team celebrates the first beam
generated at MGH in Boston, June 1997.

Adjusting the detector on the proton
therapy system at MGH, 1997.

increases. A restructuring was therefore necessary. The management, *de facto* run by Yves Jongen and Pierre Mottet as a partnership since 1990, was reluctant to lay off staff. Yet the transparency it had always shown enabled responsible negotiations on both sides. The favorable social climate allowed for an objective, collegial view of the situation. In 1993, the workforce was reduced from 144 to 115 employees, then to 87 in 1994, while ensuring that technical know-how remained intact. The accounts were cleared, and critical R&D spending was maintained. With these efforts, IBA braced itself as it waited for its tech bets to find their market.

The company's patience was soon rewarded, and by 1995, it had recovered financially. Turnover doubled in 1996. As it celebrated its tenth anniversary, management emphasized that IBA had entered a period of maturity, highlighting the risk reduction achieved through its successful diversification strategy. Revenues tripled again in 1997, still almost entirely from exports. While the markets for the Cyclone 30 and PET cyclotrons remained limited, it was mainly the sales of several Rhodotrons, along with new 18+ cyclotrons for brachytherapy—ordered in large quantities by Theragenics—that made these impressive results possible.

In proton therapy, the installation project at Massachusetts General Hospital was on schedule, even though budget was going off course. The machine was ready for delivery to Boston in 1997 as planned. To support the cyclotron, the 130-ton rotating gantries were manufactured in Wallonia by Cockerill Mechanical Industries, with an operating accuracy of about one-tenth of a

millimeter. However, developing the control software turned out to be much more challenging than expected. It involved programming nearly as complex as that of a nuclear power plant. Chief Financial Officer Éric de Lamotte, who joined the management team in the early 1990s to form a triumvirate, decided to hire a specialist company, Spacebel, which made coordination even more complicated. Yves was sent to Boston as Chief Research Officer to supervise the project, formally resigning as CEO in favor of Pierre. The thirty-member team worked in shifts, around the clock. This massive effort created a strong bond among the team members.

For its part, Sumitomo secured a contract in Tokyo that automatically impacted IBA's business. In the United States, the impending success of the new system sparked the interest of Tenet Healthcare, the second-largest hospital group in the country. Tenet placed an order for three proton therapy systems and signed an exclusive collaboration agreement with IBA, promising to take the business to a whole new level. In a chance turn of events, a fire broke out at IBA on the evening of the signing with Tenet. Yves rushed to control the fire while Pierre reassured and distracted the clients. The worst was avoided.

"We didn't know it was impossible, so we did it! Sometimes several times a day!"

- Pierre Mottet

Peril and renewal

IBA could once again hire qualified personnel and prepare for the next phase of growth. Now that the company had reached a milestone in its development, the venture capitalists who had recently invested announced their intention to withdraw. Many were skeptical that IBA could truly take off without the backing of a large group. A Boston-based investment bank was tasked with gauging the interest of industrial companies such as General Atomics, Varian, and MDS Nordion. The latter, IBA's main competitor in the sterilization market, soon put itself forward as a candidate to take control. With its older radioactive cobalt sterilization technology now threatened by the breakthrough of the Rhodotron, MDS Nordion saw an opportunity to eliminate a formidable competitor by stifling IBA's innovative ambitions.

This bleak prospect prompted a fierce reaction from IBA's management and staff, who were determined to remain in control of their own destiny. They refused to follow in the footsteps of other Belgian industrial flagships that had been sold off to foreign buyers. Pierre, who led the operation, persuaded the shareholders not to sell immediately, giving them time to weigh their options. Initial internal discussions came to the conclusion that the most legitimate owners of IBA should be its managers themselves, via a leveraged management buyout. Taking the idea further, the team decided to involve the entire workforce through a leveraged employee buyout—a formula discovered almost by chance.

The Belgabeam cooperative was established to "ensure a stable, long-term shareholder base, capable of and committed to protecting the social and economic interests of the company, its members, and its environment".[20] In addition to the shares and stock options they already held, some staff members went into debt to participate. In total, fifty-eight of the eighty-five employees, along with several board directors, took part in the takeover. At this stage, the staff were investing with no prospect of a quick exit. An informal doctrine was established that the resale of shares would occur only in exceptional circumstances. This helped foster a strong sense of proprietorship among the staff, who felt they owned the company they were working for.

Belgabeam subsequently repurchased the 62 percent of shares put up for sale, at the cost of significant leverage from Banque Bruxelles Lambert (BBL). The offer, which was marginally higher than MDS Nordion's, was completed thanks to the immediate support of IRE and Nivelinvest, with UCL joining in. The deal seemed secure until an unexpected twist: SRIW indicated that the transaction should be considered a friendly takeover, entitling it to request the purchase of its 15 percent stake. The amount of financing required exceeded Belgabeam's available resources, immediately plunging the new structure into a critical position and creating unease between the parties that would only fade much later with the arrival of Olivier Vanderijst at the head of SRIW.[21]

Cover of the Belgian magazine *Trends-Tendances* announcing the selection of the two managers for 1997, January 8, 1998.

At this point, Pierre contacted Tenet Healthcare's management, which had just committed over $100 million to develop proton therapy at its hospitals in the United States. He invited them to acquire 15 percent of IBA, provided that the decision was made, and the funds were released within the legal deadline of sixty days imposed by SRIW. A race against time ensued. Pierre spent most of the summer at Tenet's headquarters, reinforcing a strategic customer relationship in the process. By mid-September, the contracts were signed, the funds transferred, and SRIW's stake was bought out. Belgabeam was i mmediately and completely debt-free.

What had been an existential threat turned into a major opportunity, leading to a complete restructuring of IBA. The company's future was now in the hands of a shareholder base largely composed of employees committed to protecting the company's long-term future. Subsequently, careful attention was given to establishing statutes and governance mechanisms to preserve this autonomy and protect IBA from any future takeover attempts.

Yves Jongen, "the engineer who didn't want to become a manager", and Pierre Mottet, "the salesman who didn't know what a cyclotron was", were joint winners of the 1997 Manager of the Year award from Trends-Tendances magazine "for their exceptional performance at the head of IBA and their excellent complementarity".[22] The start-up soared, propelled by its remarkable capacity for innovation and the entrepreneurial spirit that empowered it to seize control of its own destiny.

ÉCONOMIE ET FINANCES 23e ANNÉE
N°1 - 2 HEBDOMADAIRE 150 F 8 JANVIER 1998
tendances
Trends
Pierre Mottet et Yves Jongen (IBA)
Managers de l'Année
Tête-à-tête : les vérités de Jean-Claude Juncker
Bourse : les 30 actions à retenir en 1998
CASH!

VERTIGINOUS GROWTH

[1998-2003]

3

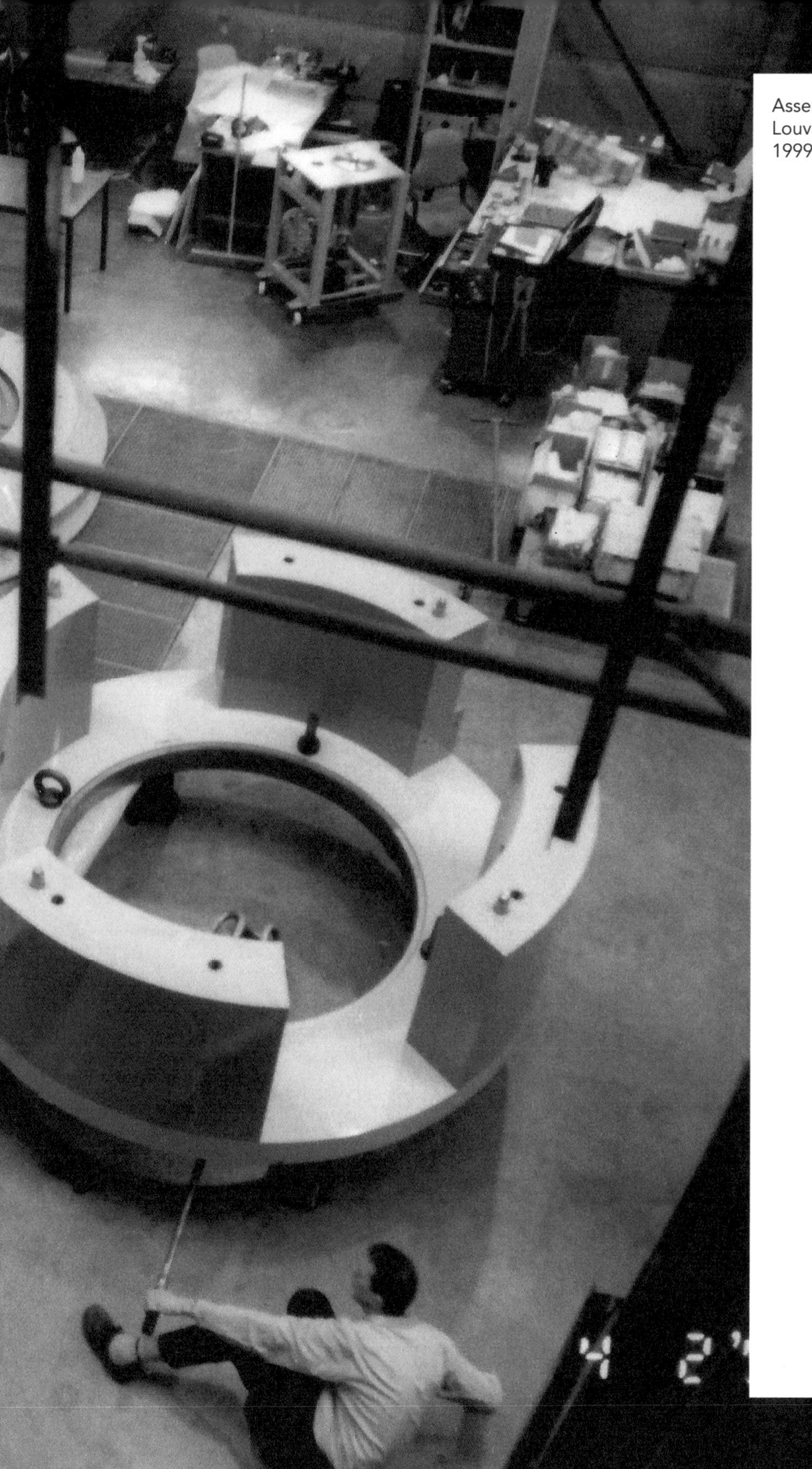

Assembly hall in Louvain-la-Neuve, 1999.

A spectacular IPO

Over more than a dozen years, IBA began to stabilize its business model, built on strategic diversification, a talent for developing new products, a fully integrated subcontracting system, and an agility that allowed it to operate worldwide—much like its sales representatives and "interventionists", who were always ready to take off at a moment's notice for impromptu after-sales missions to the far corners of the world.

At that time, IBA was established as a small technology holding company serving a broad range of markets based on its core expertise: applied physics. Since its founding, it had sold sixty-five accelerators, and its team had grown to 150 employees. This technological treasure trove drew considerable attention during a period of intense stock market activity. The timing was ideal for an IPO—an opportunity to raise new capital, strengthen its financial foundation, and support further expansion. An investment bank valued IBA at €200 million, twelve times higher than just a year earlier, when Belgabeam acquired its majority stake. Both investment bankers and emerging stock markets dedicated to fast-growing technology firms, such as EASDAQ, competed to attract IBA's interest. Ultimately, the Brussels Stock Exchange's Premier Marché was selected to help reduce the volatility and pressure typical of tech markets.

The IPO occurred on June 22, 1998, amid great enthusiasm. The entire staff was invited to the Grand Hall of the Brussels Stock Exchange, along with clients and guests. 28 percent of the shares were offered at €12, raising €15 million in initial funding. The offering was oversubscribed thirty-two times, and trading was postponed for several weeks due to a lack of sellers. The surge in orders even crashed the main bank's network. Within a year, the share price increased fivefold, fueled by optimistic market expectations, and the company's valuation soared to €1.1 billion. The stock was added to the BEL20 index, which comprises Belgium's 20 leading listed companies. This wave of excitement allowed IBA to accelerate its growth. Until then, the company had relied on creative financing for each new product line, but suddenly, capital was plentiful. This influx of funds increased pressure on management, who felt compelled to deliver the growth the market demanded, as shown by dizzying price-to-earnings ratios that reached ninety. Organic growth alone was not enough; acquisitions became necessary to keep up momentum, with banks eager to provide generous lines of credit.

At the same time, IBA's leadership took decisive steps to strengthen the company's foundation and prevent any hostile takeover bids. Belgabeam, Tenet, IRE, and UCL/Sopartec entered into a shareholders' agreement, establishing joint control through 2003. To enhance transparency and governance, the articles of association were amended to include provisions requiring disclosure for any holdings exceeding 3 percent, along with clauses on authorized capital.

Blazing a multinational trail

IBA pursued its acquisition strategy at breakneck speed, determined to position itself as a provider of comprehensive solutions in its key markets, guided by the principle of one-stop shopping. The initial plan focused on acquiring complementary companies to broaden its product portfolio, then diversifying downstream along the value chain to embrace a "functional economy"—a concept ahead of its time. The goal was to stabilize revenue streams, capture value further down the chain, secure internal outlets for its accelerators, and achieve synergies in the sale of equipment and related services.

In December 1998, IBA made its first acquisition, purchasing the Swedish company Mediflash, parent of the venerable Scanditronix—a longtime rival with whom IBA had often crossed swords but always maintained cordial relations—for €6.5 million. Olivier Legrain, a young financial controller who had joined IBA in 1996, was dispatched to Uppsala as CFO of the new subsidiary, working alongside CEO Erik Hedlund to facilitate integration. Scanditronix brought with it a portfolio of low-energy electron accelerators, known as Betaline, for sterilizing small quantities of medical consumables; 50 MeV microtrons for radiotherapy; and a dosimetry business for planning and measuring the doses of radioactive products administered to radiotherapy patients.

To support what was expected to be a period of rapid external growth, IBA launched a second fundraising campaign in March 1999. This round was also oversubscribed, successfully fetching an additional €175 million. A few months later, in May 1999, IBA acquired New York-based Radiation Dynamics Inc. (RDI), a leader in low- and medium-energy linear electron accelerators (Dynamitrons), from Sumitomo for $5 million. This transaction allowed IBA to expand its product range into new segments of the ionization market and strengthen its presence in the United States. Later that month, IBA purchased Bavarian company Wellhöffer, another major player in dosimetry for radiotherapy and diagnostics, for €9 million. Wellhöffer merged with Scanditronix's dosimetry division, positioning IBA as the global leader in the sector.

In another major move in May, IBA acquired Chicago-based Griffith Micro Science (GMS), a global leader in medical sterilization with nineteen service centers in North America and Europe, for $100 million. Then, in July, IBA completed its biggest transaction: acquiring Sterigenics for $214 million. Based in California, Sterigenics was the world leader in radioactive cobalt sterilization, operating sixteen service centers across the United States. The goal of these two acquisitions was to expand the use of the Rhodotron and gradually replace older cobalt and ethylene oxide sterilization methods. IBA became the global leader in sterilization, which quickly became its most profitable business segment, generating two-thirds of its revenue.

In just a few months, IBA experienced a dramatic transformation. Five successive acquisitions transformed a small, innovative, and agile organization into a global industrial leader. In less than six months, the group controlled more than 200 industrial systems installed worldwide. Revenue skyrocketed, tripling in a single year. The workforce expanded rapidly, growing from 150 to 1,150 employees across forty-two sites in fourteen countries. This rapid growth earned IBA the title of Company of the Year from De Tijd/L'Écho newspaper in 1999. However, this meteoric rise came with a cost: debt increased from €67 million to €352 million.

Heavily indebted, IBA returned to the market in January 2000 for a third capital increase of €170 million, just weeks before the internet bubble burst and shook the global financial system, wiping out hundreds of billions of dollars in stock market value. This time, investor interest was noticeably tepid, and share prices started to decline.

To reduce the risk of further dilution from issuing new shares and to reinforce the company's Belgian roots, amendments to the articles of association had been approved a few months earlier. These amendments notably limited voting rights and increased the threshold for approving changes. In the interest of good

IBA merged the dosimetry activities of Scanditronix and Wellhöffer in 1999, forming a global market leader.

Headquarters of Radiation Dynamics Inc. in Long Island, New York, acquired in 1999.

The Dynamitron, a linear accelerator manufactured by Radiation Dynamics Inc.

governance, a joint board of directors was established, composed of one-third management representatives, one-third major shareholders, and one-third independent directors. Jean Stéphenne (director of SmithKline Beecham Biologicals), Peter Vermeeren (former director of Mallinckrodt Medical), and Jacques de Vaucleroy (managing director of BBL Bank) contributed their expertise.

The capital increase diluted existing shareholders' stakes, resulting in the dissolution of the shareholders' agreement entered into at the IPO. Their share dropped from 57 percent to 48 percent. The Belgabeam holding, renamed Belgian Anchorage, saw its stake decline to 28.3 percent, with 6.1 percent going to UCL/Sopartec, 3.4 percent to IRE, and 10.6 percent to Tenet Healthcare. Nonetheless, an extra layer of protection was added in the form of a 'poison pill.'

Faced with rapid growth, IBA's structure needed a reevaluation. Although the collaborative model from the early days was a core principle, it was no longer sufficient to handle the increasing complexity. The two executive directors felt they had reached the limits of their management abilities. In March 2000, Jean-Claude Delobel joined as CEO from Cockerill Sambre, marking a significant management shift. Yves Jongen focused on technology, while Pierre Mottet continued leading the executive committee.

The organization became more modular through the creation of business units (BUs), each responsible for its own strategy, operations, budget, marketing, sales, distribution channels, logistics, and financial oversight. Four primary BUs were formed: Sterilization & Ionization, Radiotherapy, Radioisotopes, and a Technology Unit focused on the development, production, and servicing of accelerators. These units were supported by shared services—including human resources, finance, legal, IT, and communications—that were duplicated in

RDI

Medical consumables sterilization line in the United States following the acquisitions of Griffith Micro Science and SteriGenics, 2001.

Research and development represented 10 percent of IBA's revenue, 2001.

Europe and in the United States and billed the BUs for their use. A management team supervised the entire operation, ensuring consistency and making trade-off decisions.

Research and development (R&D) also adapted to this new reality. Under Yves Jongen's supervision, a set of guiding principles was established. Investment in R&D remained at 10 percent of revenue. Development was decentralized to stay close to the market, and only projects offering unique value propositions were selected. IBA aimed for technological leadership in each target market by providing high-end products that could justify a premium price. A selection committee evaluated projects submitted by R&D teams worldwide, fostering healthy competition. Despite internal budget battles, cross-functional cooperation was encouraged. Quality became a top priority, aligned with the ISO 9001 standard. A strict patent policy was enforced to ensure strong legal protection in case of litigation. Finally, an expert committee was appointed to identify promising ideas that did not yet fit into formal projects. In short, maintaining IBA's innovative spirit was essential.

As expected, rapid growth led to numerous integration challenges. Combining IT systems, financial reporting, and HR processes proved difficult, especially since these integrations had to be done across business units and national legal entities. The corporate culture also struggled to be consistent. Some managers of acquired companies, worried about losing their autonomy, actively resisted integration. However, these acquisitions provided valuable resources and allowed the integration of experienced executives to support the development process.

On the commercial front, IBA chose not to limit itself to equipment sales. The company invested in service centers for both sterilization and radioisotopes, positioning itself in direct competition with some of its customers who had purchased accelerators.

Amid the 2001 Anthrax threat, IBA installed an electron beam decontamination center in Bridgeport, New Jersey to process letters sent to the White House.

In the workshops, the technology unit in charge of accelerators faced the challenge of industrialization and supported all business units, 2001.

Regarding radioisotopes, the focus was on opening centers to produce and ship the valuable FDG tracer for medical imaging. Plans were made to establish sites in Lyon and Milan, and eventually across Europe. In the United States, strategic alliances were formed to quickly expand a network of centers. Meanwhile, IBA remained open to participating in special projects, such as MYRRHA (Multi-purpose hYbrid Research Reactor for High-tech Applications), a pioneering nuclear waste treatment initiative conducted with SCK-CEN. In the sterilization segment, most of the group's subsidiaries participated in a major consolidation effort. This strategy was well received by the market, supported by the growing trend among pharmaceutical companies to outsource the sterilization of medical accessories. However, competitors —most notably Isomedix—responded with a priçe war that squeezed margins. IBA also partnered with Minnesota-based Ecolab to focus on food ionization, a rapidly growing sector showing great promise as U.S. health authorities expanded the range of eligible food products. The difficult integration of GMS and Sterigenics was initially led by Kevin Swan, GMS's former CEO. When Swan left at the end of 1999, Dave Mayer, SteriGenics' second-in-command, took over. During this period, many experienced Sterigenics executives departed, and the U.S. headquarters was centralized in Chicago. Beyond the medical and food industries, electron beam irradiation opened doors to various other applications: improving semiconductors, doping precious metals, purifying water and air, drying wood, replacing chemicals used to treat textile fibers, strengthening electrical cables for automobiles, enhancing composite materials for aerospace, and even disinfecting White House mail following the 2001 anthrax attacks.

In its other business segments, IBA developed a comprehensive range of dosimetry products while continuing to industrialize its expanded portfolio of accelerators. Yet its most ambitious undertaking—the proton therapy project at Massachusetts General Hospital—turned into a financial disaster due to significant delays in software development. This was just one of the many challenges the company faced at the dawn of the new millennium.

The hangover

In the early 2000s, IBA faced a series of setbacks that severely tested its resilience and slowed its growth. The euphoria of the IPO soon gave way to the realities of rapid expansion in volatile markets.

The most significant obstacle appeared in Boston, where IT problems at Massachusetts General Hospital delayed approval by the Food and Drug Administration (FDA), and slowed the global rollout of proton therapy. Prospective clients in Korea, Taiwan, and the United States wanted to see the system in action before making additional commitments. The first patient was expected to be treated in 1998, but this milestone was delayed until three years later—seven years after the contract was signed. Ultimately, the project cost IBA €62 million, well above the initial €20 million budget. An unfavorable exchange rate for the dollar worsened the impact by an extra 20 percent. Eager to win the contract, IBA took on excessive financial risk, a move that could have bankrupted the company, as the MGH expert had warned. However, the money raised during the IPO and revenue from other products allowed IBA to stay afloat, solidifying its reputation as a pioneer in commercial proton therapy, despite the challenges.

Another significant complication arose when Tenet, a U.S.-based group undergoing restructuring due to changes in healthcare reimbursement, was forced to cut back investments and abandon its ambitions in proton therapy. The three orders placed with IBA, already in production, were canceled completely. Internally, the team concentrated on the most urgent priorities. Negotiations with Tenet were assigned to Jim Clouser, the former CEO of SteriGenics, whose charismatic leadership was viewed as crucial for navigating this challenging turning point in the U.S. market. IBA acquired Tenet's subsidiary, Proton Therapy Corporation of America (PTCA), and was now required to blend its role as a supplier with that of a technology operator. To avoid a stock price collapse, Belgian Anchorage repurchased the IBA shares held by Tenet, taking on a significant long-term loan of €54 million. While the deal was presented as an opportunity to strengthen the company's position, investors saw it as an increase in risk.[23] Despite promising operational results, the share price kept falling, losing 50 percent of its value in just a few months. With its focus on proton therapy, IBA became more dependent than ever on achieving success in this innovative field.

Soon, opportunities arose to sell partially manufactured machines to Chinese customers aiming to establish proton therapy centers in their country. In 2001, IBA decided not to renew its agreement with Sumitomo, believing it would be more beneficial to operate independently. Cash flows from other activities, especially sterilization, allowed the company to fund its proton therapy development program.

However, it soon became clear that IBA was spreading itself too thin, and tough decisions had to be made about which battles to fight. Food pasteurization, for example, although promising, did not succeed as expected. The U.S. Department of Agriculture did not approve prepared meals and meat. Competitors moved upmarket, and a rival, Titan, hindered IBA's progress through patent litigation, forcing the company into expensive legal battles.

The management team in 1999: from left to right, in the foreground: Ahmet Cokragan (Sales), Sabine de Voghel (Sales), Yves Jongen (CRO), Vivienne Gaskell (Communications), Erik Hedlund (Scanditronix), Olivier Legrain (Finance); back row: Jean-Louis Bol (Industrial), Pierre Mottet (CEO), Kevin Swan (GMS), Jim Clouser (SteriGenics), Éric de Lamotte (Finance).

Installation of the Cyclone 235, the heart of the MGH proton therapy system, Boston, February 2001.

In the medical field, IBA continued its acquisition strategy by taking majority stakes in two companies in 2001: Boston-based RadioMed, developer of a new brachytherapy implant technique for prostate cancer treatment called Radiocoil, and Eastern Isotopes. The latter acquisition allowed IBA to start producing and distributing FDG in the United States.

After becoming CEO, Jean-Claude Delobel struggled to adapt to IBA's constant uncertainty. Coming from Cockerill Sambre, where steel orders followed a steady pattern, he was not used to the instability of a groundbreaking technology company. When he asked his colleagues Pierre and Yves about their plans for proton therapy, Yves responded with a hint of defiance, "We'd like to sell a system next year. If we don't succeed, we have a redundancy plan ready. If we sell two, we won't know how to produce them, but that will be a good problem to have!"[24] The cultural divide was just too great. After commissioning a study from consulting firm Arthur D. Little, Delobel suggested to the Board that equipment manufacturing should be dropped and that the focus should be put on more stable markets, like sterilization services and radioisotope production. While the idea made sense in difficult times, it would have meant giving up IBA's core technology for the sake of stability. Pierre and Yves strongly opposed and ultimately won out after passionate debates. In early 2002, Delobel resigned, leaving outsiders stunned.

One leadership crisis after another

Jim Clouser stepped forward with a sharp and clear-eyed analysis of the company's situation. IBA's senior management believed he could turn the company around, especially since most of the group's revenue came from the United States. Listing on NASDAQ looked increasingly appealing, as comparable companies were valued higher there and had easier access to capital. Impressed by his entrepreneurial skills, the Board appointed him Chief Operating Officer (COO), while Pierre Mottet remained Chairman of the Executive Committee and, officially, CEO.

Clouser's assessment was unequivocal: IBA had world-class expertise and highly skilled teams in accelerator technology and was well positioned to succeed in related markets. The company already held a dominant market share in sterilization and strong positions in medical applications. However, heavy debt and challenges in generating cash—due to the capital-intensive development of sterilization and radioisotope centers—undermined the company's finances. Refinancing the debt proved difficult as market and bank credibility declined. Internal complexities remained a barrier, and teamwork was strained, both between Europe and the United States and among various American subsidiaries. Furthermore, the transition to industrial-scale accelerator production had not yet occurred. Reliability and quality issues began to surface, sparking discontent among some customers. Competition intensified across most segments: EBCO gained ground in the high-energy cyclotron market; General Electric and CTI occupied the mid-range; Mevex, Wassic, and Titan were present in the low- and medium-energy electron accelerator market; and Hitachi, Mitsubishi, Sumitomo, and Accel progressed in proton therapy. The Rhodotron remained unrivaled. Yet, some areas of activity—such as gamma ray and ethylene oxide sterilization—fell outside IBA's traditional core expertise. These developments raised profound questions about IBA's core identity and purpose. The technological aspect of its mission could no longer serve as a unifying force for the entire group.[25]

Jim Clouser proposed several options to restore balance at IBA: selling or spinning off various businesses, simplifying operations, reorganizing, and even relocating the group's headquarters to California. This last option meant laying off the Chicago regional headquarters team and rehiring experienced former Sterigenics executives at a premium. He urged the board to act quickly and decisively. Under his leadership, the company articulated a new mission statement: "Protect, Enhance, and Save Lives"—a motto that would endure.

The reorganization aimed to improve production efficiency and bring business units closer to customers. However, the results did not meet expectations. Belgian executives assigned to the new California headquarters struggled to collaborate with the American team. Amid a struggling stock market—still shaken by scandals at Enron, WorldCom, and Lernout & Hauspie—IBA's share price continued to decline, reaching a low of 2.6 in March 2003. At this point, an IPO in the U.S. seemed unlikely. Meanwhile, the bank's loan terms for IBA's major acquisitions were expiring, and during a global financial crisis, what was supposed to be an easy refinancing became uncertain. The only option was to sell some assets. The company's main source of income—the sterilization and ionization business—was put up for sale.

The sale of the sterilization business—acquired and developed at great expense over four years—was a painful setback. Spread across 39 locations on three continents and heavily exposed to the U.S. market, this business created most of the group's cash flow. However, this was not a return to starting point. Meanwhile, revenue from other activities increased from €20 million to €100 million, and IBA had advanced its proton therapy business. The group's exposure to the dollar was also projected to decrease from 70 percent to 30 percent after the sale—a notable change, considering the 20 percent decline of the U.S. dollar against the euro over the past year. Ultimately, the sale also meant relocating the headquarters back to Louvain-la-Neuve and shutting down the expensive California office.

Complications arose when Jim Clouser, the COO who had overseen the preparatory phase of the sale, put himself forward as a potential buyer with American financiers for $100 million—a figure well below the original purchase price. Confronted with a clear conflict of interest, IBA's board of directors immediately terminated Clouser's mandate. Pierre Mottet resumed full responsibility for general management for the second time, launching a risky recovery effort with the help of Belgian executives sent on a rescue mission to the U.S., including Jean-Marc Bothy and Thierry Hazevoets. By the end of 2003, IBA was in an unprecedented state of crisis and tension. Hopes of creating a diversified group focused on the world's most dynamic market had been shelved. Morale and confidence hit an all-time low. The group recorded an extraordinary loss of €130 million.

"We built the plane while we were flying."

- Jean-Marc Bothy

Sterilizing the wounds

Despite the prevailing gloom, this was no time for inaction. It was crucial to rally the team and rebound quickly. Determined to stay clearheaded, the management team provided an honest assessment of the situation: "The company is losing money. The sense of responsibility has declined. Strategic planning has halted. Reporting is ineffective. The financial market's perception is poor. Morale is low. Aside from that, all is well".[26] Pierre Mottet quipped to the board. An action plan was swiftly implemented: renewed financial discipline, a tighter European management team, a five-year strategic plan for each product line, more robust indicators and tools, and a return to the company's original spirit. They articulated a clear belief: the passion among IBA's dedicated team remained strong, the fundamentals of their target markets were solid, their expertise persisted, and the newly formed leadership was energized and ready to propel the company forward.

In June 2004, the sterilization business was sold to two investment funds owned by the British group Prudential for $312 million. Although the resale price was roughly equal to the original purchase price in dollars, the latter value had declined by nearly 40 percent between 1998 and 2003. Nonetheless, this amount allowed the company to repay its debts and pay a dividend of €3 per share, thereby easing the burden on Belgian Anchorage. To achieve this, the capital was reduced by €76 million. Sterigenics, for its part, successfully continued the consolidation strategy initiated by IBA by acquiring several companies in the sector, including Nordion, and was listed on NASDAQ under the name Sotera Health in 2020, with a market capitalization of $6.4 billion.

IBA could now start a new chapter on firm ground. The challenges they overcame offered valuable learning experiences. Excessive debt or heavy reliance on bank credit was no longer acceptable, even for activities with high growth potential. The streamlined management team included Pierre Mottet (CEO), Yves Jongen (CRO), Jean-Marc Bothy (CFO), Thierry Hazevoets (M&A), Olivier Legrain (Molecular Imaging), Rob Plompen and Karl Schwartz (Diagnostic and Therapeutic Dosimetry), Jean-Louis Bol (Industrial Solutions), Jean-Marc Andral (Proton Therapy, from 2007 onward), Jean-Marie Ginion (Technology), and Frank Uytterhaegen (China). A process of deep reflection led to a more practical approach to the markets and a reaffirmed vision.

MISSION AGAINST CANCER

[2004-2012]

4

STOP

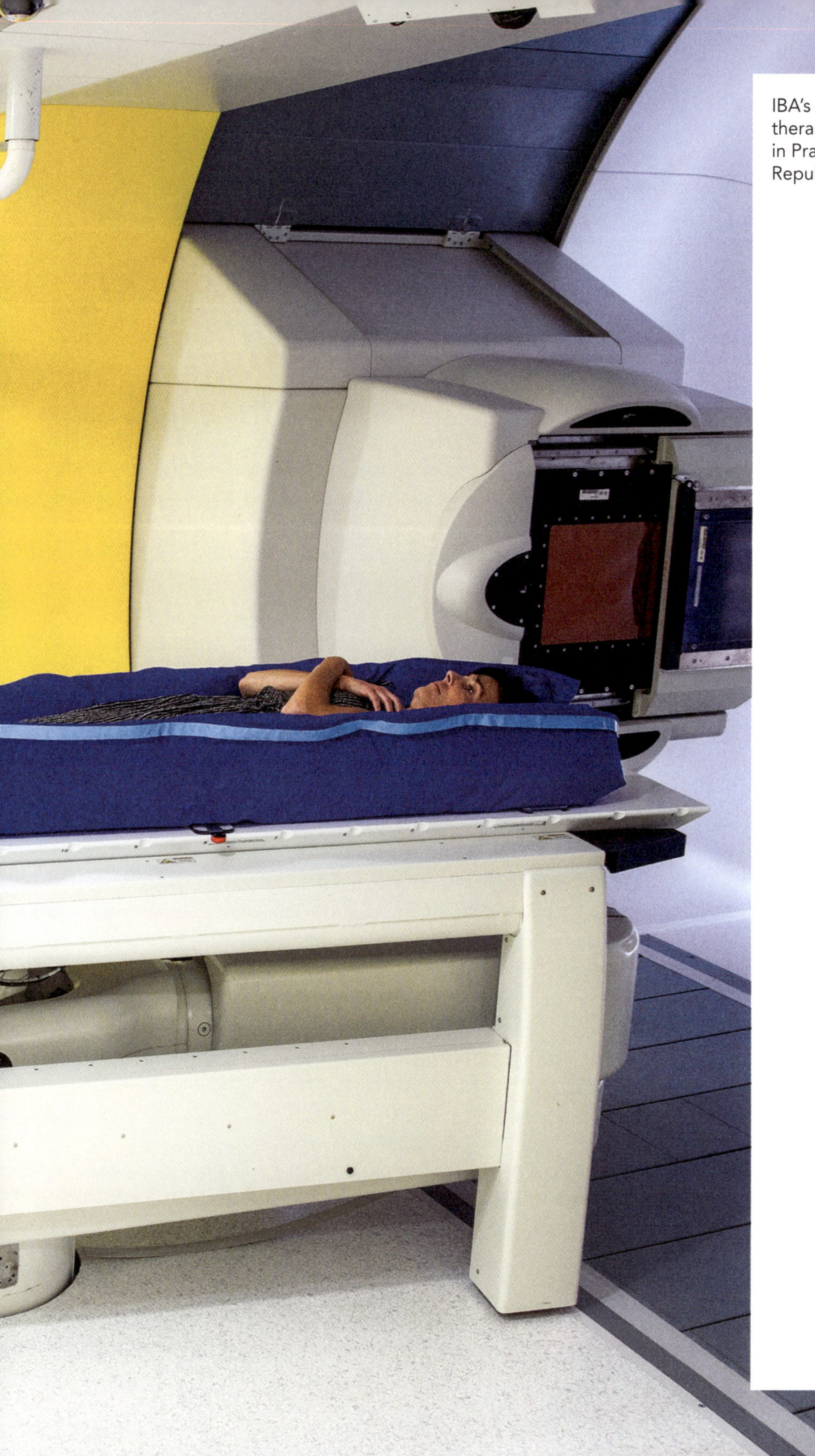

IBA's proton therapy center in Prague, Czech Republic, 2017.

Healing the world

The years 2004 and 2005 marked a profound renaissance for IBA, transforming its identity, strategy, organization, and operations. This period was not just a turning point—it was a reawakening of purpose.

With the introduction of the Belgian Corporate Governance Code, IBA seized the opportunity to formalize and publicly share the principles that would guide its future. Two foundational beliefs were set forth. First of all, entrepreneurship must be recognized as the engine of success. Secondly, shareholders should both embrace and acknowledge the ins and outs of IBA's purpose when investing in the company. It was clearly stated that IBA's success stemmed from its dynamic entrepreneurial culture—a culture that enabled the company to identify market needs and respond with intelligent solutions faster and more effectively than its competitors.

It was considered essential that IBA's teammates share this vision and feel empowered to pursue it with passion and diligence. The results would even improve for all stakeholders when everyone embodied the company's four core values: Care, Dare, Share, and Be Fair. These four core values—introduced for the first time during this period—have remained the foundation of the company's culture for decades. The company finally recognized that its ultimate goal is not just to generate short-term profits but to satisfy customers, shareholders, employees, and the communities in which it operates.[27] This was the first time IBA clearly articulated its "stakeholder approach".[28]

While management refrained from explicitly stating that shareholder enrichment did not take precedence over other objectives in the years immediately following the IPO, its stance subsequently evolved with greater confidence. This shift reflected the founders' philosophy and the teachings of Philippe de Woot, a pioneer of corporate social responsibility in Belgium who championed moral reflection on technological innovation. In 2004, de Woot stepped down as chairman of the board of directors, making way for Peter Vermeeren.

Whereas the previous era emphasized diversification—sometimes at the expense of clarity—the new strategy centered on fighting cancer by harnessing the company's unique expertise in diagnostic and therapeutic radiation. The radioisotope sector was designated as the engine of growth, marking a decisive shift in focus.

This strategic realignment required a thorough understanding of every aspect of cancer care and the patient journey through treatment. Hospitals and oncologists preferred integrated solutions over standalone devices. Software became a vital part of these solutions, prompting IBA to broaden its core expertise beyond hardware. At the same time, radiotherapy represented only one modality among many in cancer treatment. While hospitals invested heavily in radiotherapy, the pharmaceutical industry promoted chemotherapy, which was instantly reimbursed by social security systems. The competitive landscape in oncology was therefore vast and complex, demanding clear communication and education for diverse audiences—including policymakers and institutions.

Highlighting the importance of efficient, innovative, and customer-focused research and development, IBA made R&D a strategic priority as part of its commitment to delivering superior products and solutions. Past years had shown that when efforts in this area were relaxed, IBA lost significant ground to competitors. In its early days, R&D and production operated as separate units, leading to communication and transfer issues between them. By the end of the 1990s, these functions merged, introducing new challenges—such as managing both recurring and non-recurring projects within one organization and mobilizing R&D to resolve issues in the installed base. Under Jean-Claude Delobel, production became more professional but also more rigid, and research on accelerators was pushed to the background. In 2004, a reversal happened to reintroduce flexibility into R&D, empowering project managers to oversee their projects through the early stages of production.

In the new organization, product and application R&D primarily fell to the business units. A small team at the central level oversaw the entire process, managed patents, and identified sources of regional and European subsidies. While fundamental research was left to academic institutions, IBA aimed to stay close to them to quickly transfer results to industry. To achieve this, partnerships were maintained with several universities.

Under Yves Jongen's supervision, the organization remained heavily dependent on the founder's expertise. A succession plan was put in place with a 2012 deadline. However, none of the candidates met all the required qualifications, and initial attempts to develop young talent's skills fell short. This issue became a recurring theme. Indeed, this field is highly specialized, and the need for experts in accelerators, software development, radiochemistry, product integration, cost optimization, and other disciplines was constantly growing. Fortunately, Wallonia and Belgium boasted an abundant pool of engineers and scientists. The diversity of cutting-edge professions IBA offers attracts experts in superconductivity, nuclear energy, vacuum technology, magnetism, automation, digital technology, biology, and nuclear chemistry. The next challenge was to retain them.

IBA devoted particular attention to enhancing the "employee experience" by introducing recognition programs, incentives, training opportunities, and career development within a stimulating and meaningful work environment. While employees were paid in line with market rates, there were ample opportunities for growth, especially for engineers seeking technical challenges. Not to mention the fun and gratification of working in a motivating atmosphere, which have remained tangible hallmarks of IBA's culture over the years.

Another aspect that set the company apart was its customer relationships. IBA aimed to lighten their burden, treat them as it would like to be treated, prioritize their needs in its R&D programs, and expose as many employees as possible to customers so they could better understand their concerns. This approach had become somewhat diluted by its expanded activities, but it was once again prioritized. Because of its innovative and disruptive nature, IBA regularly had opportunities to deliver untested machines—sometimes prototypes—to early-adopter customers. The company co-innovated with pioneering buyers, including MGH, Medi+Physics, Stüder, and Theragenics. In each case, IBA earned their trust "by resolving problems to their complete satisfaction", thereby building its reputation.[29]

Although the US market still made up 30 percent of sales, its significance declined geographically. Focus shifted to China, which was becoming the "world's factory". With its growing economy, China also represented a large domestic market. Like most medical equipment manufacturers, IBA established a commercial presence there early on and explored technological partnerships. This time, IBA took a further step by setting up a PET cyclotron production plant in Beijing in 2007. The goal was to produce standardized machines at lower costs within the dollar zone. However, the experience proved less than ideal, due to the complexity of coordinating engineering in Louvain-la-Neuve with production in China and the challenges of developing software locally. Nevertheless, IBA could not afford to ignore this opportunity.

The realignment process also involved a comprehensive review of product lines and the identification of target markets. IBA's goal was to become or stay among the top one or two competitors in each selected market. The two main focus areas were proton therapy and, more importantly, molecular imaging.

After the merger of the Swedish and German companies, the integration of the dosimetry division was successful. This core activity became a profitable and stabilizing addition to IBA's portfolio, offering insight into the conventional radiotherapy industry. The division was named Best Supplier of the Year by Siemens six times within eight years.

Opening of the new production site in Beijing, China. Frank Uyterhaegen and Pierre Mottet show Walloon ministers Jean-Claude Marcourt and Marie-Dominique Simonet around the premises, 2006.

The 2005 annual report introduced a new visual identity, symbolizing IBA's rebirth focused on the fight against cancer.

Yves Jongen supervising the installation of the proton therapy center at MGH, when the University of Florida team came to survey the site, 2001.

Traditional cyclotron and electron accelerator sales stayed steady in increasingly uncertain markets, where saturation effects often followed major sales. Most cyclotrons were exported to developing countries entering the nuclear medicine field, including India, Turkey, and Vietnam.

Despite the recognized quality of Radiocoil radioactive implants, brachytherapy did not become widespread after IBA entered the market through the acquisition of RadioMed. Palladium-103 was gradually replaced by iodine-125 produced in nuclear reactors. This effort was discontinued in 2006, except for Visicoil technology, which is designed to produce non-irradiated gold helical implants used to locate tumors during radiotherapy treatments. This product line became a major commercial success for IBA, demonstrating that, "as long as the story isn't over, you never know whether you've won or lost".[30]

To grow without relying on acquisitions, IBA strengthened its partnerships across all business sectors, collaborating with both industrial and institutional partners. This was particularly evident in molecular imaging and proton therapy, but also in dosimetry. Examples include partnerships with Turin's Institute of Nuclear Physics to develop the new I'mRT MastriXX dosimeter and with the Swedish software company Raysearch to create quality assurance solutions for radiotherapy.

iba

The race for proton therapy dominance

In the world of proton therapy, IBA's hard-won success in Boston established the company as a pioneer. The crisis caused by Tenet Healthcare's withdrawal in 2000 led to the cancellation of three planned sales. However, this setback was offset by two contracts signed in China in 2001—one with Wanjie Tumor Hospital in Zibo and another with the Chang An Group in Xian—followed by a third contract with Korea's National Cancer Center in 2002. Equipment already manufactured for Tenet was reassigned to these projects, reducing the time between construction and treatment start. Despite this, the business remained unprofitable and artisanal, with a strong focus on research and development. Software stability was still hard to achieve. Generating sales was essential to creating a virtuous cycle that could transform the business from a fragile venture into a viable enterprise.

The call of Florida

Meanwhile, advances in commercial proton therapy gained the attention of the University of Florida College of Medicine (UF Health). In 2000, Nancy Mendenhall, who led the Department of Radiation Oncology from 1993 to 2006, persuaded her superiors to start the first project of its kind in the southeastern United States. Discussions commenced with Loma Linda University and its technical partner, Optivus, about installing a single-room system. However, UF Health soon questioned Optivus's ability to develop critical new features such as Pencil Beam Scanning (PBS). After ending their commitment to Optivus, UF Health officials visited the center under construction in Boston, where IBA was installing its system. The beam was being produced but was hard to control. The officials met Yves Jongen, who was working on the cyclotron in the vault. They immediately connected. IBA was no longer represented by Tenet, which helped build a trusting relationship. Nancy Mendenhall and her colleagues were quickly convinced that IBA was the right partner to ensure the project's success because, as they put it, "for IBA, it's not just business; it's passion. They listen deeply and put the patient at the center. They share the same goals as doctors".[31]

Frustrated by this reversal, Optivus then filed a lawsuit against IBA for infringing on five of its patents. After six years of litigation, the California court ruled in IBA's favor, recognizing the originality of its technologies. After spending millions of dollars on legal fees, the parties agreed to settle the dispute. Meanwhile, negotiations with the University of Florida took a long time due to the still-fragile economic climate. The contract was finally signed in January 2004, thanks to a structured financing solution that minimized risks for both parties. The center opened in Jacksonville in the summer of 2006, two weeks ahead of schedule.

From craftsmanship to small-scale production

IBA repeatedly proved to be a dependable supplier. The company successfully built two centers simultaneously in Florida and Korea, each on a site the size of a football field with two dedicated teams. 2006 marked a turning point, as four new contracts were signed with the University of Pennsylvania, the Curie Institute in Orsay, France, the University Hospital of Essen in Germany, and the private company ProCure in Oklahoma.

The support from the Belgian export agency (ONDD), led by Yves Windelinckx, proved essential. The ONDD had been involved since the start of the MGH project and helped organize and secure financing for complex projects lasting several years. The proton therapy business was too large and risky to be included in IBA's annual balance sheet or to be supported by traditional banks.

Revenue from each project was recorded on a pro rata basis as it advanced. This demanded strict discipline in managing expenses. Each center represented an investment of around €100 million, with half allocated to the technology supplier. Typically, a sale took four to five years to materialize, depending on the healthcare system. Private projects targeted profitability in the United States. China was under state control. Japan had a national preference. European

Advertisement in the early 2000s promoting the superiority of proton therapy, particularly for treating children.

IBA building China's first proton therapy center, Wanjie, in Zibo, Shandong Province, 2002.

Frank Uyterhaegen exploring prospects at the National Cancer Center near Seoul, Korea, 2002.

public healthcare systems were cautious with their budgets. Yet one thing remained certain: "The only certainty for every project is that it will be delayed".[32] This proved challenging to handle for a company with such a passionate and enthusiastic spirit.

Despite these challenges, proton therapy gradually became more common. An active community of users started to form. IBA recognized the importance of boosting its marketing and communicating its innovations not just to the Particle Therapy Co-Operative Group (PTCOG) but also to a broader audience at events like conferences of the European Society for Radiotherapy and Oncology (ESTRO) and the American Society for Radiation Oncology (ASTRO), which attract thousands of professionals. IBA made a strong impact by lighting public displays in IBA green in Jacksonville, turning traffic lights green along the route taken by Wanjie participants, and renting an aircraft carrier to showcase its products at ASTRO. The in-house rock band, the "Zizotopes", performed at the event. As Minister Wathelet summarized, "IBA is know-how, know-how-to-tell, and know-how-to-let-know".[33]

To meet demand, IBA initiated a bold industrial expansion plan to produce equipment for up to eight centers annually in Louvain-la-Neuve. The target was two to three sales per year, but this capacity was adjusted to handle order surges. Under the leadership of Jean-Marc Andral, a former operations director at General Electric, the business unit expanded from 50 to 400 employees. He introduced industrial discipline and increased the R&D budget to 12 percent of the group's total revenue, setting a new standard.

Precision, his only chance.

When there should be minimal tolerance for side effects, proton radiation therapy is your best option.

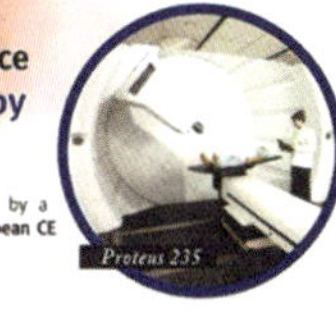

IBA's proven Proteus 235 has been carefully reviewed and selected by a number of leading institutions in the world. It is **the only FDA and European CE cleared** proton radiation therapy system available.

IBA: Leading the Way in Proton Precision.

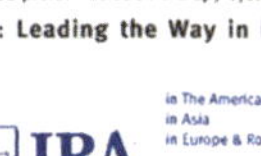

in The Americas : Chris Chandler ❑ tel: +1 502 426 2108 ❑ e-mail: cchandler@iba-group.com
in Asia : Frank Uytterhaegen ❑ tel: +86 136 0109 3702 ❑ e-mail: frankuytterhaegen@ibachina.com
in Europe & Row : Volker Schirrmeister ❑ tel: +49 170 44 66 567 ❑ e-mail: Volker.Schirrmeister@iba.be
Marielle Demilie ❑ tel: +32 495 58 68 28 ❑ e-mail: Marielle.Demilie@iba.be
www.iba-worldwide.com

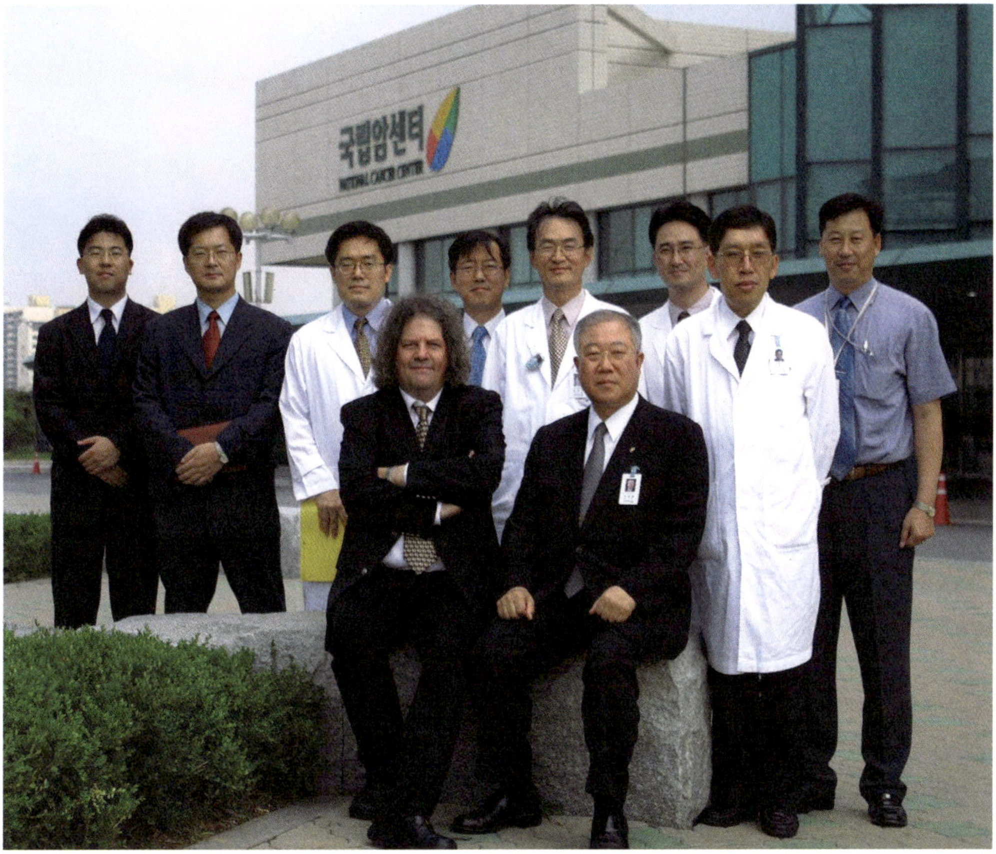

Weaving a web

In 2007, IBA established a strategic partnership with ProCure, an American company that aimed to standardize proton therapy through a private clinic model. The Oklahoma City center, which opened in 2009, reflected this goal. It was the first center worldwide to use an inclined beam instead of a rotating gantry, allowing for a more compact and cost-effective design. This collaboration continued with centers in Chicago, built in 24 months, and two others in Somerset, New Jersey, and Seattle, built in 12 months. ProCure created a scalable model structured as a network of private clinics funded by investment groups. IBA played a key role in this model by providing equipment, engineering, integration, and maintenance. This turnkey approach was designed to reduce lead times, speed up return on investment, and increase access to proton therapy.

The main advantage for IBA was the ability to establish a viable business model. Equipment sales now included ten-year operating contracts worth several million euros per center annually, with guaranteed uptime, which was essential for the centers' bank financing. These arrangements laid the foundation for stable, long-term recurring revenue.

Beyond the partnership with ProCure, American centers were planned for Knoxville, Tennessee, and Shreveport, Louisiana. In Europe, several countries selected IBA for their first steps in proton therapy, including the Czech Republic, Italy, Russia, Poland, and Sweden.

Lord of the ring

While IBA dominated the scene with over 50 percent market share, competition began to increase. Although data remained limited, early independent studies estimated that about 15 percent of patients receiving radiation therapy could benefit significantly from proton therapy—especially children and young adults, for whom conserving healthy tissue is essential.[34] The potential market appeared promising.

In 2006, Varian, the global leader in conventional radiotherapy, began discussing a partnership or joint venture with IBA. This alliance could have given IBA significant commercial power; at the time, Varian had 4,000 employees and generated $1.6 billion in revenue. The California-based company also supplied IBA's software. However, negotiations were halted in 2007 when Varian gained direct market access by acquiring Accel Instruments, a German firm near bankruptcy, for $30 million. In response, IBA signed a commercial agreement with Elekta, the second-largest radiotherapy company worldwide, as well as with CMS, for developing Treatment Planning Systems (TPS).

Hitachi expanded beyond Japan and established a presence at the MD Anderson Cancer Center in Texas by accepting payment only from patient billing, which IBA could not afford to do. After considering a partnership with IBA, Siemens chose to develop hadron therapy equipment independently—a more complex and costly version of proton therapy that the German company hoped would treat more patients. In the United States, the startup Still River (later Mevion) introduced a compact, affordable system based on a superconducting synchrocyclotron—a solution subsequently adopted and enhanced by IBA. Therefore, IBA continued independently, facing larger competitors.

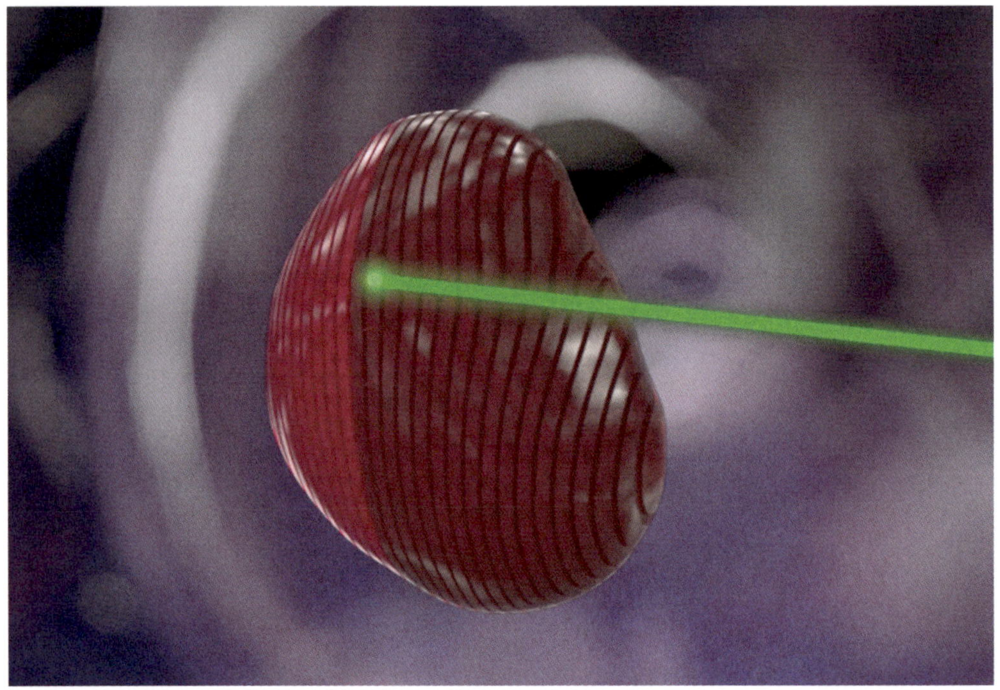

The IBA team posing in the metal structure of the rotating gantry at the University of Florida Proton Therapy Center in Jacksonville, 2005.

Pencil Beam Scanning (PBS) allows the beam to "paint" the tumor millimeter by millimeter, minimizing exposure to surrounding healthy tissue.

Racing with innovation

Throughout the first decade of the 21st century, proton therapy underwent a major technological advancement, becoming a standard clinical treatment. The most significant development was the introduction of Pencil Beam Scanning (PBS), which offered unmatched precision in dose delivery. This technology allowed tumors to be 'painted' precisely, millimeter by millimeter, reducing exposure to surrounding healthy tissue. PBS paved the way for Intensity-Modulated Proton Therapy (IMPT), a dose-shaping technique that enables exact adjustment of the dose to match the tumor's three-dimensional shape. Although the Paul Scherrer Institute (PSI) in Switzerland first demonstrated PBS in the 1990s, it was not used clinically until 2005, with an accelerator supplied by Accel. IBA created an early proof of concept for PBS in 2000, working closely with the Massachusetts General Hospital team, and received FDA approval in 2008. The first treatment with PBS was performed in Boston on December 23, 2008.

Beyond this essential function, IBA continued to innovate to enhance the accuracy and accessibility of treatments. Between 2009 and 2012, the company perfected beam scanning and robotic patient positioning. It integrated advanced imaging software and automated safety systems, enabling remote maintenance of its facilities and allowing diagnostics and updates from Louvain-la-Neuve. Significant progress was also achieved in motion management and real-time imaging, with coordination facilitated by integrating Elekta and Varian software. Most notably, in 2010, IBA announced the ProteusONE concept: a compact, affordable system poised to transform the proton therapy industry.

Meanwhile, hadron therapy using heavy carbon ions and other lighter ions instead of protons marked a breakthrough in the academic world. First tested in the 1970s, this technique proved especially effective in treating radio-resistant tumors with complex shapes. However, its technical complexity and high cost limited its use. After discussions with Siemens in 2004, IBA realized it needed to incorporate this technology into its product range to stay ahead in the market. IBA quickly saw that its proton therapy systems could be modified to produce carbon ions. In 2006, IBA introduced the idea of a "two-step particle therapy design" at ASTRO. Two years later, IBA partnered with Archade, a collaboration between the François Baclesse Center and Caen University Hospital in France. The partners started a long-term project where IBA would supply a brand-new, 400-MeV superconducting isochronous cyclotron for hadron therapy—the largest ever built by IBA. But in 2011, Siemens decided to withdraw from its venture after experiencing heavy losses in particle therapy. This gave IBA the opportunity to continue its work in the field at a slower, more cautious pace.

In this environment of growing technological and commercial competition, proton therapy moved beyond academia and permanently entered an industrial phase characterized by system miniaturization, advanced treatments, and rivalry for access to worldwide hospital markets.

"While financial efficiency and performance are both necessary and valuable, IBA's purpose is to fight cancer and contribute to the well-being of society."

- Pierre Mottet

The radiopharmaceutical vision

The promise of a fast-growing market

Proton therapy is IBA's flagship achievement, showcasing its innovative spirit in particle accelerator technology. However, in 2004, the bold strategic shift toward oncology pushed molecular imaging to the forefront of IBA's goals. This field, driven by scientific breakthroughs and the potential for rapid growth, became the company's main driver of expansion. By that time, IBA had already secured a strong position in molecular imaging, leveraging its expertise in cyclotron design for radioisotope production. These radioisotopes powered both SPECT (Single Photon Emission Computed Tomography)—an accessible and widely used imaging method—and PET (Positron Emission Tomography), a more advanced technique essential in oncology, neurology, and cardiology.

IBA's flagship cyclotrons, the Cyclone 18/9 and Cyclone 30, were continuously improved, reflecting the company's dedication to innovation. Alongside these, IBA delivered high-quality targets. However, the company identified a key gap: it fell behind in automated chemical synthesis systems, a crucial part of the radiotracer production process. Jean-Luc Morelle, who led the development of IBA's first synthesis modules, left in 1994, feeling his contributions were undervalued. He later founded Coincidence, which was acquired by General Electric, and in 2004, he launched Trasis—a company poised to lead in radiopharmaceutical synthesis technology. Recognizing its deficiency in chemistry, IBA responded firmly. In 2006, it introduced Synthera, a new line of synthesis devices providing an all-in-one solution that covered the entire process—from cyclotron to injectable dose.

FDG was the most commonly used tracer for PET scans. Its use grew rapidly in the United States, propelled by expanding Medicare reimbursement. Europe soon followed this trend. While some hospitals opted to produce FDG on-site, most depended on regional production centers, each serving several facilities within roughly 100 kilometers. This approach developed due to a key physical limit: fluorine-18's half-life of about 110 minutes requires quick, coordinated logistics for production, quality control, and distribution. In this environment, a unique opportunity arose for companies capable of creating large networks of radiopharmacies. IBA was determined to take advantage of it.

A combination of scale and speed

IBA's entry into the industrial radiopharmaceutical sector started in 2000 when it opened its first radioisotope production facility in Lyon and acquired Eastern Isotopes, a U.S. company specializing in FDG production. At the time, this acquisition was still a minor part of IBA's portfolio, which was mainly focused on sterilization services. However, it gave the company a strategic foothold in the U.S. market and valuable expertise in managing for short-lived isotopes. Well-positioned geographically, this network served as a springboard for future growth in a quickly expanding U.S. market, where competition was increasing. In Europe, joint ventures followed in 2002 and 2003: in Belgium with the Saint-Luc University Clinics, and in the U.K. with pharmaceutical group Schering, to establish new production centers. As part of this strategy, IBA's longstanding partnership with the IRE proved to be another important asset.

Starting in 2004, IBA began a drive to expand its geographical network and deliver FDG doses as quickly, safely, and traceably as possible. This growth was fueled by alliances, acquisitions, and in-house development, requiring significant human, financial, and organizational resources. Beyond just increasing volume, this approach was driven by the expectation of a major shift: the generic FDG market was anticipated to move toward a multi-tracer model featuring molecules targeting specific diseases or cell types. IBA's core strategy was to build a functional distribution network that would become crucial when the new generation of proprietary tracers reached the market.

Olivier Legrain, who became president of this business unit, summarized the priorities: "For the U.S., it's about expanding the network through external growth to achieve global reach and prevent competitors from creating zones of profitable monopolies that would allow them to attack us with aggressive pricing in our markets. For Europe, it's about consolidating existing activities and continuing development on a country-by-country basis. The overall objective is to be number one or two in each market. In research and development, the division must anticipate the development of new molecules and adapt its offering accordingly".[35]

Once again, IBA confidently faced off against industry giant Siemens, which adopted a similar strategy since its 2005 acquisition of long-time partner CTI, which operated 43 FDG centers in the U.S. through its subsidiary PETNET Solutions. Expansion proceeded rapidly: IBA's network grew from 16 sites in 2003 to 35 in 2006, 40 in 2008, and up to 54 operational sites in 2011, spanning three continents. This growth increased the group's total workforce to 2,200 employees in 2011, with half of the workforce working in the molecular imaging business unit.

CIS Bio International: a transformative acquisition

In 2006, IBA made a significant move toward vertical integration by acquiring Schering AG's radiopharmaceutical operations. Included in this transaction was CIS Bio International, a major player in European radiopharmacy. Founded in 1990 as a spin-off from the French Atomic Energy Commission's historic work at the Saclay site, CIS Bio grew to employ about 600 people, and generated annual sales of roughly €120 million. Its portfolio covered a wide range of medical conditions—oncology, cardiology, neurology, and endocrinology—supported by a broad selection of SPECT and PET tracers. The company also operated a bioassay unit dedicated to developing biomarkers for in vitro diagnostics and drug discovery.

At the time of acquisition, CIS Bio faced major challenges. Its SPECT production facility in Saclay needed extensive renovations, and the company was barely profitable and heavily in debt. Schering recapitalized CIS Bio with €65 million before offering it for sale at a symbolic price of €1. For IBA, the opportunity was compelling: to acquire an operator with both industrial and pharmaceutical capabilities and to strengthen its position in the European FDG market.

To finalize the deal, IBA formed a consortium with the Institut National des Radioéléments (IRE), represented by Henri Bonet and Nicole Destexhe, who had previously supported IBA's 1997 employee buyout. IRE took an 80 percent stake in CIS Bio, while IBA held the remaining 20 percent. The initial plan was to split the activities: IRE would oversee the SPECT portfolio, and IBA would handle PET and FDG distribution. However, labor resistance quickly arose as CIS Bio unions opposed the split, forcing IBA to negotiate directly with them. Once the deal was completed, joint governance with IRE proved unfeasible. IBA's minority stake limited its ability to manage the PET business with the necessary flexibility. Meanwhile, management recognized that renovating the Saclay plant, though challenging, was technically and economically feasible. IBA then decided to buy out IRE's stake and take full control of CIS Bio, paying with IBA shares and strengthening IRE's position as a shareholder in IBA.

The integration process was daunting. IBA had to add 600 new employees to a team already around 1,000 strong. The corporate cultures were very different, but over time, a new integrated division formed, combining IBA's FDG production activities with CIS Bio's regulatory and commercial expertise.

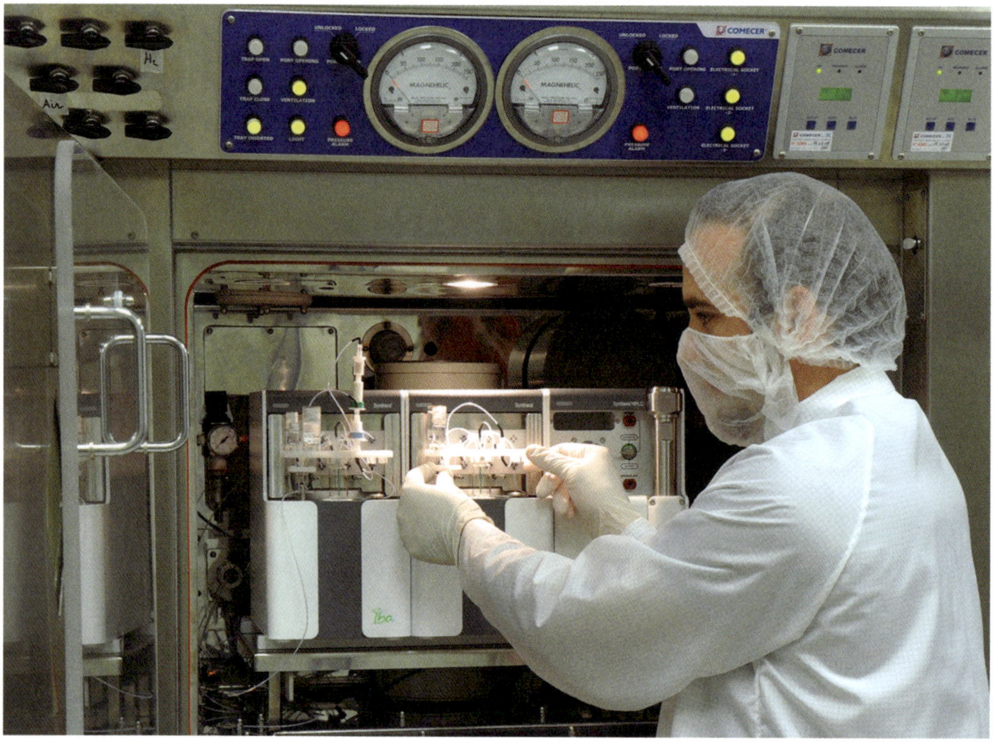

COMECER
UNLOCKED
LOCKED
TRAP OPEN
PORT OPENING
TRAP CLOSE
VENTILATION
TRAY INSERTED
LIGHT
PRESSURE ALARM
MAGNEHELIC
MAGNEHELIC
UNLOCKED
LOCKED
PORT OPENING
ELECTRICAL SOCKET
VENTILATION
ELECTRICAL SOCKET
PRESSURE ALARM
ELECTRICAL SOCKET
COMECER
COMECER

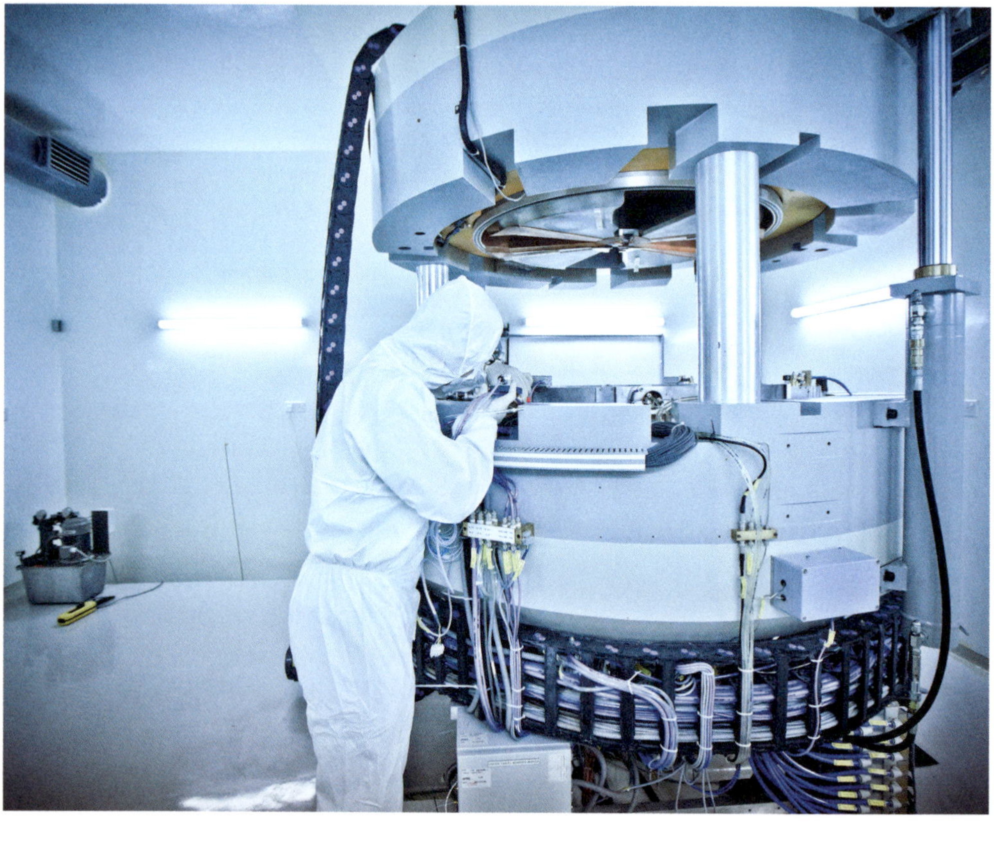

The Synthera automated chemistry system enables the production of injectable radioisotope doses at the treatment site, 2010.

Maintenance of a Cyclone 18/9 in a sterile room in Malaysia, 2011.

This acquisition transformed IBA into an integrated biotechnology company, entering the demanding pharmaceutical industry, which includes preclinical research, clinical trials, intellectual property strategies, and negotiations with health authorities. It paved the way for a new strategy aligned with nuclear medicine: developing proprietary molecules.

From generics to molecular innovation

The development of IBA's FDG production and distribution network, which started in 2000, was just the beginning. Early on, IBA recognized that the future of radiopharmacy depended on access to patented molecules, enabling personalized medicine and advanced diagnosis.

In 2006, the company formed a dedicated team to identify, license, or develop innovative molecules. The initial targets focused on unmet medical needs: prostate cancer, Alzheimer's disease, and apoptosis—programmed cell death, which serves as a valuable indicator of a tumor's response to treatment. These projects required a notably different timeframe: longer development cycles, higher investments, and more acute risk management compared to a generic product like FDG.

IBA's ambition went beyond just producing these molecules to also co-owning the innovations themselves. Through exclusive licensing agreements, the company aimed to secure market access and establish itself as a player in clinical development. This strategy was supported by two key strengths: its global network of centers and its technical expertise in radioactive labeling.

Production of FDG at the Cliniques universitaires Saint-Luc, Belgium, 2008.

This new direction quickly developed through a series of partnerships. In June 2008, IBA signed a global agreement with the German company Wilex AG to distribute Redectane, a diagnostic imaging agent used to distinguish benign from malignant kidney tumors. In August of the same year, IBA partnered with the Israeli biotech firm Aposense to radiolabel and distribute a tracer for visualizing apoptosis. By August 2010, the company signed a contract with Bayer to co-develop a molecule capable of detecting Alzheimer's disease.

Through CIS Bio and its own research, IBA aimed to develop a portfolio that would distinguish itself—not only in oncology but also in cardiology and neurology. However, these efforts required significant investments, which directly competed with funding for proton therapy and other product lines.

A strategy under pressure

The simultaneous growth of two business lines—technology and pharmaceuticals—raised internal questions about whether to keep these activities under a single governance structure. This strategic consideration became more urgent in a rapidly changing economic environment. The 2008 financial crisis limited several external growth initiatives, increased financing costs, and complicated contract negotiations. Although the group's revenue grew a remarkable 15 percent annually from 2005 to 2010, driven by acquisitions in molecular imaging, net income and cash flow declined.

By 2010, the molecular imaging business unit had generated €217 million in revenue, up from €37 million in 2004. It grew sixfold over six years, fueled by continual investment and evolving into a more complex business model. Its share of the group's revenue increased from 31 percent to 56 percent. However, this numerical growth masked certain vulnerabilities. The initially promising FDG market was quickly becoming commoditized. In both the United States and Europe, the sector was shifting toward a price war and a low-cost model emphasizing logistical efficiency and cost-cutting. Prices fell, and margins narrowed. Additionally, the proprietary molecules still carried uncertain long-term risks.

Approximately €100 million would be needed over five years to remain competitive. IBA secured a €50 million loan from the European Investment Bank, but financing all of the group's activities at once would have been risky during the subprime crisis, which limited credit availability. These factors led IBA to consider structural solutions.

In 2009, the concept of splitting was introduced. The goal was to assign each division an appropriate governance structure, specialized investors, and a clear financial plan. Similar to the sale of the sterilization division in 2003, it seemed impossible to detach from the core business focused on accelerators. Various options were considered for the molecular imaging business unit: sale, IPO, or joint venture. Once again, IBA prepared to divest its largest revenue-generating business, which was capital-intensive and had evolved from a downstream diversification strategy that led it to compete with its own customers. The project codenamed "Star Wars" was initiated. It involved establishing a joint venture with a major industrial firm to consolidate the sector. Negotiations dragged on before finally concluding in 2011. In a last effort, IBA acquired a 25 percent stake in Siemens' German PETNET network, securing exclusive distribution rights for Bayer products at a significant financial cost.

An ambition unfulfilled

In 2011, IBA adopted a new strategy. The company formed a strategic partnership with SK Capital Partners, a US-based investment firm specializing in life sciences. The agreement involved selling a 60 percent majority stake in the molecular imaging business unit for €75 million, while IBA kept the remaining 40 percent. This move was both strategic and practical: it allowed IBA to free up capital while maintaining a stake in the company's future growth. It also enabled the radiopharmaceutical division to become an independent entity with its own growth goals, resources, and management team. Olivier Legrain, who had served as president of the division and was about to become CEO of IBA, handed over leadership to Renaud Dehareng in 2011. Dehareng led the restructuring of the molecular imaging business and oversaw its final spin-off from IBA's portfolio in 2016, after selling the minority stake for €30 million to private investment fund CapVest. With new funding sources and a renewed focus on operational execution, Dehareng continued the strategy initiated by IBA. After acquiring Mallinckrodt Nuclear Imaging, he established the Curium group, which became a global leader within ten years, reaching a valuation of €6 billion in 2024.

Reflecting on these events, Olivier Legrain noted: "Given IBA's remarkable potential to develop new markets in sterilization and nuclear medicine, we probably did not fully capture all the value we could have legitimately aimed for. One of the factors influencing this decision was our desire to retain control of the Group. When you exclude any capital increase on principle, the only way to fund growth is to turn to the banks, and we accepted that choice".[36]

Another factor was the lack of access to sufficient financing. With a new CEO leading the company, IBA needed to reinvent itself for the second time in ten years, sharpening its focus on its core business: accelerators for medical and industrial applications. The era of unlimited external growth had ended, at least for now.

GROWING FROM THE HEART

[2012-2017]

5

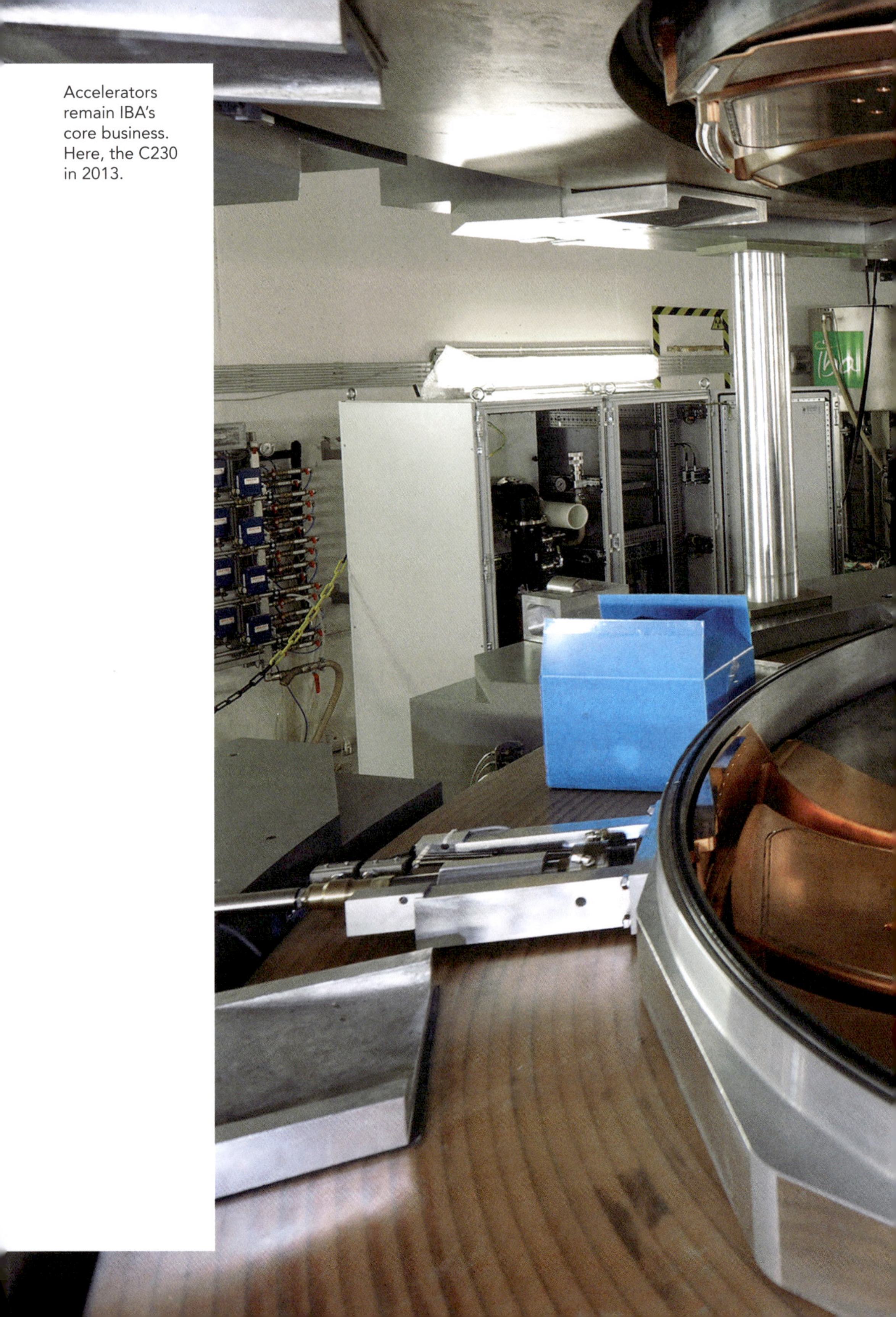

Accelerators remain IBA's core business. Here, the C230 in 2013.

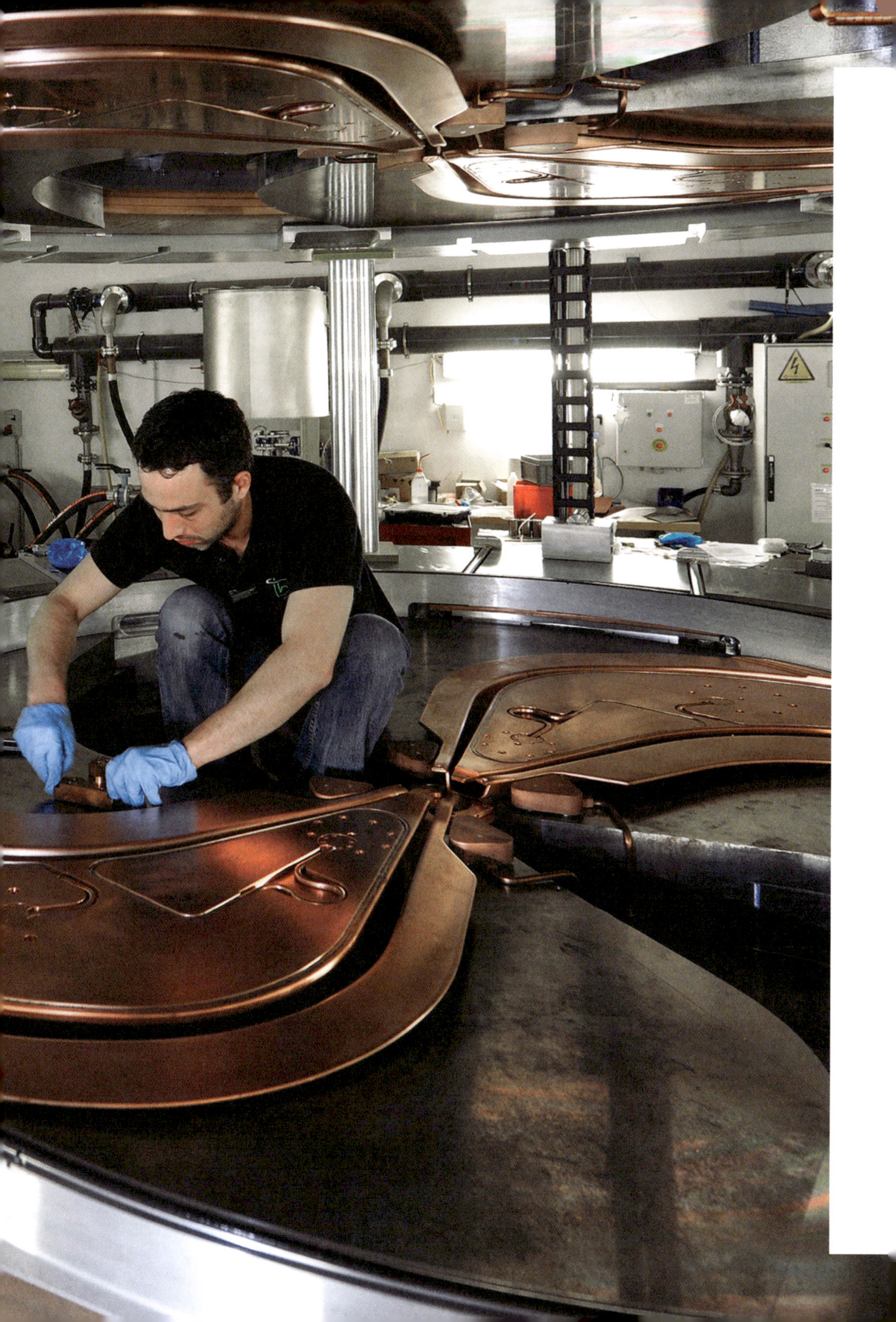

Passing the baton for a new chapter

For the second time in its history, IBA became streamlined after shedding a significant part of its business and revenue. The pharmaceutical journey, which would take several more years to fully complete, left both a scar and a valuable lesson. IBA was repositioned as a MedTech company, with medical technology at its heart.

Although accelerators remained at the heart of IBA's expertise, they also became a barrier to developing other downstream activities. Whenever two divisions competed for resources, technology always took priority. It formed the heart of IBA and established the company as a global leader in three key areas: proton therapy, dosimetry, and high- and medium-energy accelerators. IBA's leaders had the responsibility to leverage this expertise, and so far, dosimetry was the only acquired activity to show consistent success over time. Could the solution ultimately be to become a pure player and seize well-chosen opportunities along the way?

The United States and France, the two countries with the highest number of employees, fell back into line. The global workforce shrank from 2,200 to 1,100 people. Once again, Louvain-la-Neuve reestablished itself as the group's hub, particularly since the production of Cyclone 18/9 machines was moved from China back to Belgium. Despite its longstanding international outlook, IBA often revisited its roots to recharge and prepare for future growth.

Similar to the previous crisis, IBA proved highly vulnerable to fluctuations in the global economy. The 2008 financial crisis, like that of 2001, stifled markets and tightened credit and financing conditions. The company's finances were once again in a fragile state. Credit lines were exhausted, proton therapy client funds were mostly tied up in intangible assets while contracts were being fulfilled, and bad news from Essen could even knock IBA out of the ring.

The Essen proton therapy center project, signed in 2006, was meant to mark a historic milestone for IBA. It was not only the company's first system in Europe and one of the largest in the world, but also the first project to be part of a public-private partnership. IBA teamed up with construction firm Strabag to deliver a turnkey center and provide maintenance for fifteen years, with a total budget of €300 million, including €50 million for equipment. The IBA-Strabag consortium took on unlimited liability for the whole project. Construction went as planned, and the four treatment rooms were finished on time. However, after the infrastructure was completed, disagreements emerged during the handover of the center. The management of Essen University Hospital, which had changed since the agreement was signed, argued that the specifications in the call for tenders were binding, not those in the contract. IBA insisted that it had met its obligations by passing the acceptance tests outlined in the contract. The court ruling in Germany was unfavorable to IBA. In 2012, the company had to set aside €28 million to cover potential losses and lost the confidence of one of its main banks, BNP Paribas Fortis. IBA appealed the ruling while negotiations continued, but meanwhile, costs kept rising. The Essen center, meant as a commercial showcase in Europe, became a symbol of the risks involved in large-scale turnkey projects.

In this unstable environment, Olivier Legrain prepared to succeed Pierre Mottet as CEO of IBA. Two previous attempts to appoint an external CEO had failed. This time, it was clear that the company needed someone from within—someone familiar with IBA's specific business, deeply rooted in its culture, who had faced past existential threats, and demonstrated the ability to grow the business while maintaining financial discipline. Olivier Legrain fit these criteria, having started as a financial controller in 1996 before leading the dosimetry division in Sweden and the molecular imaging division in the United States.

It was agreed among Olivier, Pierre, and Yves that after spending a sabbatical year sailing around the world with his family, Olivier would take control of IBA. In May 2011, as his sailing boat arrived at the Caribbean island of Turks and Caicos, the three men met to discuss the extent of freedom and flexibility Olivier would have alongside the two long-standing executives, who remained firm in their desire to oversee IBA's future. The powers were clearly defined: Olivier would make all decisions regarding day-to-day management, consulting with his predecessors only on strategic directions and perimeter changes. Since Yves and Pierre were the main shareholders of Belgian Anchorage, together they represented IBA's major investor. A transition process was established. It was agreed that Pierre would continue handling the contentious Essen issue, develop a sustainability policy for IBA, and serve as its ambassador in political and economic circles. Yves kept his position as Chief Research Officer, as his successor had not yet been chosen. In this new setup, the relationship within the trio developed harmoniously over the years, based on the principle—also upheld within the Board—of being "demanding when all is well, and supportive when things go wrong".[37]

Olivier Legrain's priorities fell into two categories: restoring financial balance and giving greater responsibility to the business units. "I wanted to have people who would wake up every morning thinking about how to make their product line profitable",[38] he later recalled. The painstaking rebalancing process took four years, during which time revenue stabilized while profitability and cash flow recovered, driven by the rise of proton therapy. R&D efforts remained high, with one-fifth of staff and 12 percent of revenue reinvested. In 2013, a compromise was reached with Essen Hospital, which agreed to take over the center at a reasonable price. Market capitalization, which fell to a low of €260 million in 2011, rose to €550 million in 2014. A strong order book and increasing recurring revenues from services and maintenance inspired confidence in the future. In proton therapy in particular, the first centers that were installed reached the end of their warranty period and began generating revenues about 10 percent of their sale price. Time was on IBA's side: the strategy based on revenues from the operation and maintenance of sites was paying off. Underlying trends favored IBA.

"Everything
has become larger,
but the 'virus'
is still there...
a pioneering spirit,
passionate energy,
and the alchemy
between meaning
and technology."

- Olivier Legrain

The *IBA Sailing Team* raises funds for cancer charities, 2016.

Fueling the fire of sustainability

When Pierre Mottet became Chairman of the Board of Directors in 2013, he outlined a vision for his role: "to facilitate the continuity of the company and its creation of value, both financial and societal. While financial efficiency and performance are necessary and valuable, IBA's purpose remains its fight against cancer and its contribution to society's well-being. The company's noble mission is a unique source of motivation for all stakeholders".[39] This deeply rooted, overarching goal of creating value for all stakeholders was soon turned into a comprehensive plan and measurable initiatives.

While customers, patients, employees, and shareholders were always central to the project, the company's environmental and social commitments now required greater attention. Pierre Mottet was determined to ignite a new momentum. He sought advice from Sybille van den Hove, one of IBA's earliest employees and then chair of the Scientific Committee of the European Environment Agency. Pierre's perspectives on sustainability, like those of Olivier Legrain, crystallized when the United Nations published its Millennium Development Goals in 2000.

Beyond any formal process, Pierre launched an appeal to all employees interested in improving IBA's social and environmental impact. Participants could dedicate up to 15 percent of their time to this initiative. A €50,000 budget, personally funded by Pierre, was set aside to turn the best ideas into reality. Instead of the ten or so participants expected, eighty people attended the launch meeting. Clearly, the topic resonated with many team members.

The example set and sincere approach of the former CEO created energy and inspired employees to achieve great results. Five self-organized thematic "green cells" analyzed issues and suggested areas for improvement. Most initiatives had a return on investment of less than a year and did not even require using the proposed fund. A grassroots movement was born.

To move forward, the approach needed to be structured and integrated into the company's processes, including product design, energy consumption, purchasing, logistics, human resources, and more. A first sustainable development program was formalized in 2015, based on a star approach in which each branch represented a stakeholder. The four entities listed in 2004 were expanded to include the environment. The goal was to internalize negative externalities by implementing technical, organizational, and financial solutions to reduce or offset environmental impact: measuring externalities, improving product design to decrease energy use, enhancing building efficiency, reviewing industrial processes, raising employee awareness, promoting soft mobility, and protecting biodiversity around the sites. It also involved collaborating with organizations committed to helping the community and future generations.

A new phase in sustainability efforts began in 2017. The United Nations Sustainable Development Goals served as the reference framework, with each organization encouraged to adapt them to its specific context. After consulting all stakeholders about their most urgent concerns, IBA integrated the initiative into all parts of its operations, adopting a systemic approach with a target date of 2030. The company made a clear commitment and even aimed to lead by example, stating its intention to "widely promote an economic model that enables it to serve society profitably while drastically reducing its negative impacts".[40]

The top stakeholder priorities were the accessibility, comfort, quality, and safety of IBA's products, followed by customer satisfaction, awareness of proton therapy, and business ethics.

Based on this analysis, priorities were established for each stakeholder group. For customers and patients, the focus was on democratizing access to technology, guaranteeing total quality, and building strong partnerships.

For employees, IBA promised to provide a secure, rewarding job where everyone could innovate, succeed, and take responsibility while upholding the company's values. A "zero impact" strategy was introduced, aiming for excellence in environmental, health, and safety standards. Continuous training goals were also increased.

Regarding the environment, the initial focus was to carefully assess the impact of operations and products throughout their entire life cycle, including climate effects and radioactive waste, and to take action where it would be most effective. For example, it became clear that the electrical insulation in Dynamitrons had a significant impact, despite its small volume: SF_6 is a gas 24,000 times more potent than CO_2 in terms of greenhouse effect. A replacement technology was quickly pursued in collaboration with the University of Manchester and General Electric.

IBA's commitment to society involved partnering with organizations focused on cancer prevention, patient and family support, and improving access to treatment reimbursement. The company supported numerous initiatives in these areas, both from foundations and employees. It also actively promoted education and training through collaborations with various stakeholders, including the Foundation for Future Generations, the École Polytechnique de Louvain, UCL, and the All4Youth program.

Finally, regarding shareholders, IBA committed to delivering financial performance in line with their contributions, while aiming to involve shareholders "who share its values and ethics". Purely speculative investors clearly did not constitute the core target group.

In terms of governance, ethical principles, commitment, and integrity were upheld at all levels of the organization. Through a charter, the board of directors committed to considering all stakeholders in the corporate strategy. Gender equality was also considered, although the existing disparity in technical professions made it challenging to achieve balance. Following Nicole Destexhe of the IRE, who joined the board of directors in 1991, other women were appointed to enhance diversity: Mary Gospodarowicz (2012), Katleen Vandeweyer (2013), Sybille van den Hove (2015), Hedvig Hricak (2017), and others. In the management team, Soumya Chandramouli became the first female Chief Financial Officer in 2016, followed by Catherine Vandenborre in 2025.

Each employee was expected to sign the code of business conduct to uphold ethical standards. The risks inherent to the company had already been analyzed and listed in the annual report since 2005. In 2017, IBA published a second report on "non-financial activities". The company continued to make progress across all aspects of sustainability in an iterative, enthusiastic, and rigorous way.

ProteusONE, the winning breakthrough

When Olivier Legrain took over IBA's leadership in 2012, a key strategic goal emerged: to establish proton therapy as the primary driver of the group's growth by expanding this technology beyond its niche and establishing it as a recognized standard of care. IBA already had a portfolio of more than 73 installed or planned rooms across 25 centers worldwide, accounting for over 50 percent of the market share—more than all competitors combined. Over 20,000 patients had been treated using IBA equipment, demonstrating the company's impact. However, globally, only about 1 percent of radiotherapy patients had access to proton therapy. IBA set an ambitious, almost provocative goal of increasing this figure to 20 percent within twenty years. This inspiring target became the strategic guide for the business unit. To reach this goal, IBA recognized the importance of convincing medical professionals and decision-makers through comprehensive clinical data. The Clinical Affairs department was established and, from 2015 onward, began publishing a series of white papers to highlight the clinical benefits of proton therapy. IBA assumed a leadership role, drawing on models such as the Dutch approach to collecting and sharing comparative data from both clinical studies and digital simulations.

A second approach involved developing adaptive proton therapy, which allows treatments to be adjusted as they progress, and hypofractionation, which shortens treatment duration by increasing the dose. Beyond technology, it was essential to leverage IBA's unique network of users, sharing experiences, protocols, and innovations with newcomers. Finally, the company strengthened its strategic alliances with key industry players: Elekta for information and planning systems, RaySearch for adaptive calculation and oncology information, and Philips for precision imaging, planning, and room ambiance. These collaborative approaches became key features of the IBA style. Unlike its main competitor,

Initial concept for the ProteusONE, 2013.

AdaptInsight CBCT software for patient positioning prior to proton therapy treatment, 2014.

Varian, which offered an all-in-one solution, IBA focused on an open architecture capable of interfacing with many non-proprietary systems. These long-term alliances would evolve as each partner's positioning developed.

Meanwhile, the commercial organization restructured itself: five main regions were established to better serve the markets—North America; Latin America; Europe, the Middle East, and Africa; Russia and neighboring countries; Asia-Pacific. Distribution agreements were signed with Toshiba for Japan and with Philips for other regions.

However, the heart of change beat elsewhere: in the workshop that created ProteusONE. Based on a design by Yves Jongen, ProteusONE was his latest major contribution to medical technology. Announced in 2010 and approved by the FDA and the European Union in 2014, this compact solution aimed to make proton therapy more accessible. This breakthrough focused on developing a new type of accelerator, the superconducting synchrocyclotron (S2C2), which was the first of its kind at IBA. The use of superconducting coils greatly reduced the machine's size—its diameter was roughly half that of the Cyclone 230, and it weighed 3.5 times less. This compact design, combined with a single-room treatment approach, significantly lowered both installation and operating costs, reducing overall financing needs. Moreover, the system featured cutting-edge PBS and IMPT capabilities. It was designed to operate reliably without an operator and to keep recurring costs low. Another key innovation was its passive extraction system, which simplified the process. These technological advancements made ProteusONE a compact, affordable solution poised to revolutionize proton therapy. Smaller and quicker to install—just nine months in the UK, setting a world record—it broke every rule in the book. Its first patient was treated in Shreveport, Louisiana, three months ahead of schedule.

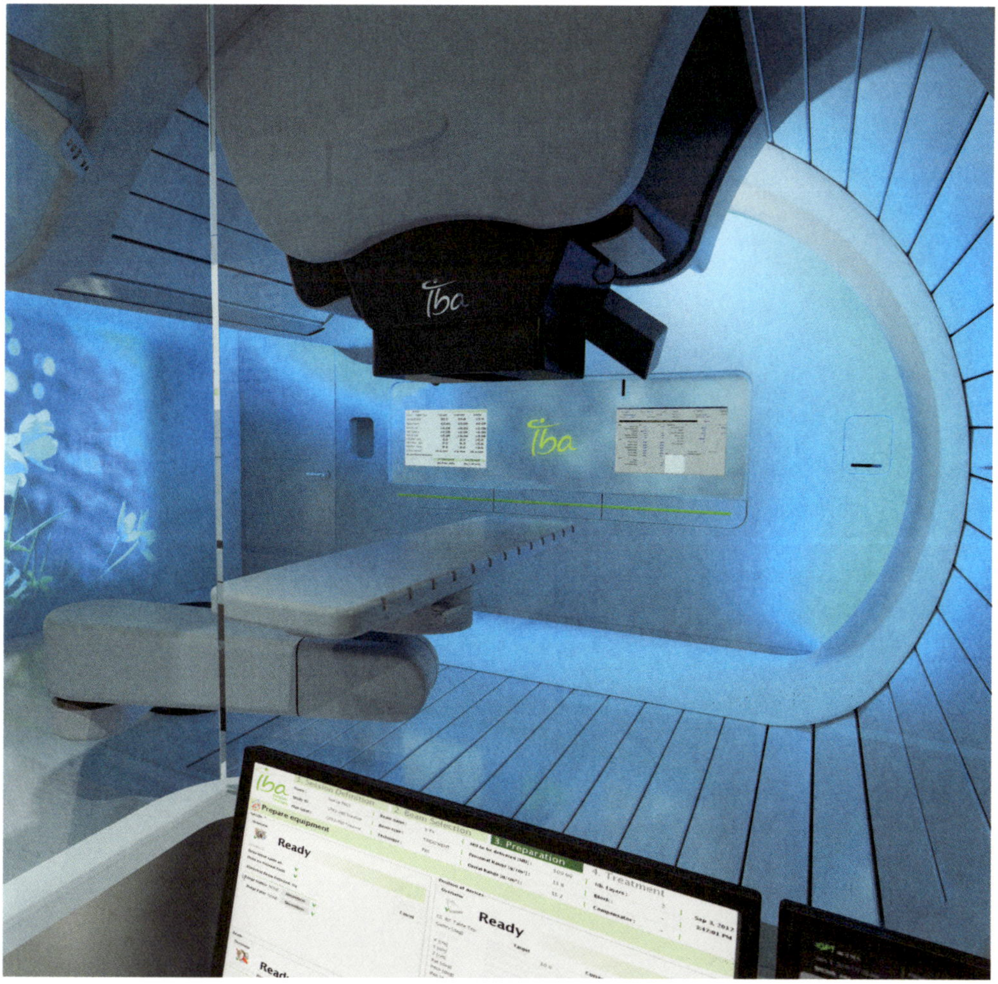

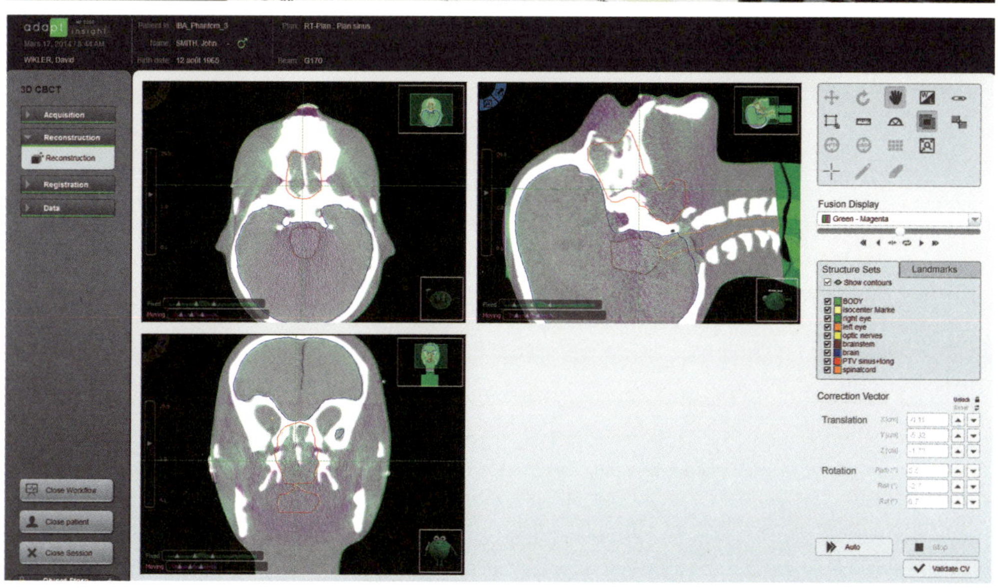

IBA_Phantom_3
SMITH, John
12 août 1965
RT-Plan : Plan sinus
G170
WIKLER, David
3D CBCT
Acquisition
Reconstruction
Reconstruction
Registration
Data
Close Workflow
Close patient
Close Session
Fusion Display
Green - Magenta
Structure Sets
Landmarks
Show contours
BODY
right eye
left eye
optic nerves
brainstem
brain
PTV sinus+long
spinalcord
Correction Vector
Translation
Rotation
Auto
Stop
Validate CV

Between 2014 and 2016, contracts poured in from countries like the Netherlands, China, United Arab Emirates, Japan, India, France, and finally Belgium, where Flemish Leuven won "the proton therapy war"[41], much to the frustration of the Walloon political sphere, which was also competing. In China, plans were announced for the world's largest proton therapy center in Zhuozhou, featuring five treatment rooms around the original ProteusPLUS system. The partnership with Philips led to the detection and integration of Cone Beam Computed Tomography (CBCT) to improve patient positioning—a world first. Momentum grew in the scientific community, with 311 studies published in 2015 and 629 in 2017. New types of tumors were targeted: head and neck, left breast, esophageal lung, spinal cord, pelvis, and more.

Although development was still in progress, ProteusONE's order book for 2015 alone reached an impressive €400 million, including service contracts. Potential sales identified exceeded €1 billion. Amid these promising prospects, double-digit growth guidance, and a dividend commitment of 30 percent of profits, the share price increased, pushing market capitalization to €1.4 billion in 2016.

IBA drove sustained growth with its internal Accelerate program—refusing to back down against its strong American competitor. In partnership with McKinsey, the initiative involved appointing a dedicated Chief Operating Officer, expanding regionalization of installation, services, sales, and marketing, hiring 600 highly-skilled professionals over two years, and building a new factory in Louvain-la-Neuve capable of assembling 20 to 30 accelerators annually, up from 8 to 10. This second major expansion at IBA's historic headquarters resulted in eight buildings housing half of the company's 1,500 global employees. Having moved beyond craftsmanship in 2007, IBA was ready to adopt large-scale production.

Innovation from top to bottom

While proton therapy drew most of the group's attention and resources, the ambition for IBA's other business units remained strong. The new CEO's roadmap clarified that the strategy for these divisions was never meant to focus only on financing proton therapy. Now that IBA was refocusing on its role as an equipment manufacturer, maintaining innovation across all business lines became essential.

Behind the proton, the electron

The Industrial Accelerators business unit had been sidelined since the forced sale of the Sterilization division in 2003. It accounted for about 10 percent of annual revenue and employed roughly 80 people across two locations: Louvain-la-Neuve and Long Island. Compared to the dominant presence of proton therapy within the company, it struggled to gain visibility internally, especially given the fluctuations in its markets. After the reorganization that started in 2004, IBA shifted its focus. Jean-Louis Bol, who was president of the division from 2005 to 2015, aimed to allocate more resources to his team to better connect with customers—a goal he largely achieved. This trend was reinforced by the reaffirmation of the role of business units beginning in 2012.

Radiation Dynamics Inc., the American subsidiary acquired in 1999, continued to produce Dynamitrons, low-energy linear accelerators mainly used to improve polymers for the automotive industry. The high-energy Rhodotrons were being built in Louvain-la-Neuve. Both teams operated with little synergy or integration, mainly due to a recurring "not invented here" syndrome at Louvain-la-Neuve. Still, these two complementary and high-performance systems enabled Industrial to offer a wide range of e-beam products. Interestingly, sales varied: usually, two Rhodotrons were sold in one year, followed by two Dynamitrons the next.

iba
iba

The Rhodotron TT1000 converts electron beams into X-rays on demand, 2009.

Industrial served a wide range of markets, viewing them as opportunities as they emerged. The Rhodotron, a device significantly more powerful than its predecessors, enabled unique applications such as biological decontamination —especially effective in treating mail sent to the White House during the anthrax scare. There were also plans to use it in the oil industry, where electron flow could reduce reliance on chemicals in oil refining. In the United States, a long-term project started in 2006 and launched in 2016 aimed to streamline cargo ship inspections at the Port of Boston and improve detection of nuclear threats. The Dynamitron was used to precisely cut silicon wafers for the photovoltaic industry in California. Unfortunately, these last three projects ultimately proved unsuccessful.

The vision from the early 2000s to penetrate the sterilization market and change it from within—replacing traditional methods like ethylene oxide and cobalt—still had not come to fruition. Major industry resistance and regulatory hurdles related to requalifying equipment kept the advanced electron irradiation technology from gaining more than 10 percent of the market.

A more technical reason for the slow adoption of Rhodotron in sterilization was the limited penetration of electrons into the matter, while the cobalt method allowed entire pallets to be irradiated. To address this, X-rays needed to be emitted. However, due to the low electron-beam conversion efficiency, the power had to be increased from 100 to 600 kW. This request was made by Canadian IBA product manager Arnold Herrer to the R&D team led by Michel Abs, the "father of the Rhodotron". The TT1000 was developed by a small team, regardless of customer orders. The device was designed to convert the powerful electron beam into X-rays on demand. Still, potential customers remained skeptical about the benefits of investing in this technological behemoth to

IntegraLab, an integrated radiopharmacy solution, 2014.

Installation of the Cyclone 70 at the Arronax center in Nantes, 2008.

replace cobalt, which, although more dangerous and subject to supply uncertainties, was well established in industry practices. Thanks to a partnership signed in 2008 with long-standing Swiss customer Leoni Stüder, the TT1000 was developed and stabilized, demonstrating the machine's efficiency and profitability. Despite this, the device was slow to gain acceptance. In 2013, it was launched under the name Rhodotron Duo, and in 2014, Mediscan in Austria became the first customer to purchase one for sterilizing medical devices.

Other initiatives were launched to expand market share, especially as other companies, including Chinese firms, began entering the e-beam equipment market by copying the Dynamitron. In 2012, Industrial started developing a product differentiation strategy and positioned itself as a sterilization systems integrator—a tactical approach adopted by IBA across all its business units to create greater value. In 2016, the TT50 at 10 MeV—a new compact system with lower energy consumption—was added to the lineup. By this time, over 250 IBA electron accelerators were in operation worldwide, including those commissioned 50 years earlier.

Towards integrated radiopharmaceutical solutions

IBA's experience as a manufacturer of radioisotope production and distribution centers gave it a strong advantage in managing every aspect of building such facilities. The business unit responsible for manufacturing medical cyclotrons—Radiopharma—used this expertise to develop comprehensive, turnkey solutions covering all project stages. Since 2013, IBA has not only sold acce-

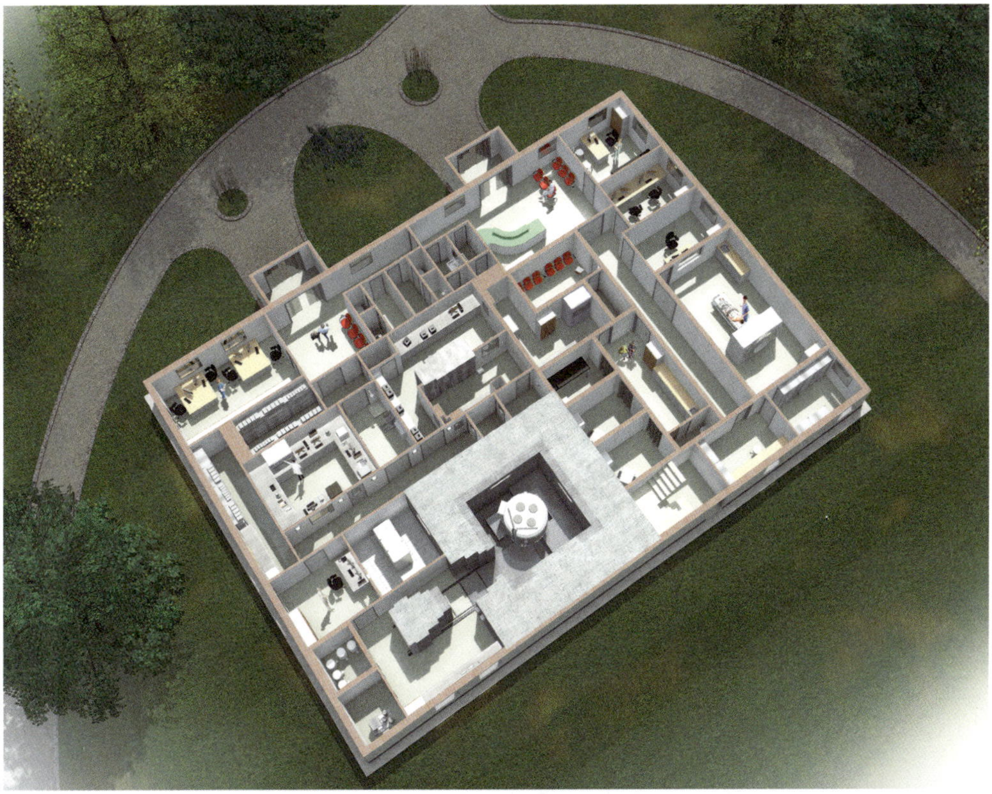

lerators to radiopharmaceutical companies but also marketed a full range of services under the name IntegraLab. By then, IBA had already installed over 200 radioisotope accelerators and sold 330 Synthera chemistry modules. As developed markets matured, IBA shifted its focus to emerging regions where nuclear medicine was growing: China, Brazil, Argentina, Chile, Uruguay, Cuba, Azerbaijan, Myanmar, Libya, Lithuania, Belarus, Mexico, Egypt, Russia, Brunei, and others.

Beyond FDG, the emergence of new radioisotopes has greatly transformed the field of nuclear medicine. IBA played a pioneering role in this change as a technical service provider for the Arronax project in Nantes. Launched in 1998 by leading academic and hospital partners, this innovative initiative started utilizing IBA's expertise in 2005. It involved designing a high-energy, high-intensity 70 MeV multiparticle cyclotron—capable of accelerating protons, alpha particles, and deuterons—to produce rare and strategic radioisotopes such as copper-64, strontium-82, and iodine-124, all crucial for new imaging techniques. It also produced astatine-211, one of the most promising alpha emitters for targeted cancer therapy. This shift toward therapeutic radioisotopes opened a new chapter for IBA's cyclotrons, which had previously been used only for diagnostic purposes. In 2009, the system was delivered to launch the research program. This technological breakthrough resulted in the Cyclone 70 cyclotron, a globally unique model that established IBA as a leader in the high-energy market. This innovation quickly gained international clients, as seen when Cyclone 70 was sold in 2013 to Zevacor in the United States and in 2014 to Russia, for use in cardiovascular disease diagnosis.

In IBA's laboratories, innovation also focused on refining existing models, continually testing the limits of physics and offering the widest range of cyclotrons on the market for both industrial and experimental use. The central R&D

department is renowned for its relentless drive to explore: "The art of management lies in allowing this creativity to express itself while imagining ways to convert it into profitable models".[42] Drawing on lessons learned from the Arronax project, IBA developed the Cyclone 30XP, a multi-particle evolution of its iconic Cyclone 30 model. The Cyclone 3 was revamped, while the self-shielded Cyclone 11 marked a milestone in the evolution of the classic Cyclone 10.

In 2016, a new standard was established with the launch of the Cyclone KIUBE—a compact, scalable, and environmentally designed cubic cyclotron capable of expanding production capacity in stages, effectively doubling productivity. Developed in close partnership with Belgian mechanical engineering firm Karl Hugo, the successor to the Cyclone 18/9 was an immediate commercial success and even displaced Siemens from this crucial market segment. Over six years, 101 units were sold, making this market killer IBA's new cash cow. Remarkably, this was achieved without any involvement from Yves Jongen, as the R&D teams performed independently.

Dosimetry: an asset under scrutiny

Between 2012 and 2018, the Bavaria-based dosimetry business unit experienced fluctuations, reflecting shifts in the global radiotherapy market. With strong operational performance and annual sales making up one-fifth of total revenue, this unit contributed to the company's financial stability. Although the accessories sold by this unit differed significantly from the large equipment marketed by IBA's other divisions, dosimetry remained closely aligned with the core mission: improving cancer diagnosis and treatment through instruments that measure radiation doses and calibrate machines.

The Cyclone KIUBE, a new standard in the radiopharmaceutical industry, 2016.

IBA's Blue Phantom dosimetry device, 2014.

This niche activity depended heavily on a strong capacity for innovation. In 2014, the company sold the thousandth unit of its flagship product, the Blue Phantom—a water or gel-filled tank lined with sensors that mimic the human body's absorption properties. Building on this flagship product, the business unit expanded its range of hardware and software solutions, employed by more than 10,000 users worldwide. These innovations met the increasing safety requirements for patients and healthcare professionals, while adhering to stricter quality assurance regulations. Progress in digitalization and electronics technology, such as real-time dose visualization, paved the way for major breakthroughs. Alongside its products, IBA reinforced its commitment to customers by launching the CAREprogram service portal, calibration services, and training courses through the International Competence Center. Together, these solutions established IBA's dosimetry range as the gold standard in technology, ensuring patient safety at every stage of care.

Competition in this sector was fierce, with IBA, the well-established German firm PTW, and the new American leader Sun Nuclear dominating the market. Discussions of consolidation were ongoing, and by 2016, the industry's future remained uncertain. The question of whether to continue this activity in the group arose, all the more true since dosimetry would gain from being provided by an independent operator.

To infinity and beyond?

By the end of 2016, euphoria had spread throughout every level of the company. The new management team had cultivated a growth-focused approach centered on the core business, with proton therapy serving as its flagship. IBA had matured organizationally and strengthened its leadership across various business lines. Innovation had delivered remarkable results. These successes were clear in widespread recruitment, the announcement of increased industrial capacity, and a stock price at its peak—"priced for perfection".

When the 2016 results were presented in March 2017, optimism remained high: with a healthy order book, revenue growth for 2017 was estimated at 15–20 percent. However, in May, an initial warning was issued: the completion of several projects had been delayed due to setbacks at customer sites. What initially seemed to be a minor hiccup in a well-oiled machine turned into a trend reversal. In July, a second profit warning was met with severe market and analyst reactions—"hangover", "stock market turmoil", "excessive optimism". By mid-year, the proton therapy business unit was €30 million below its forecasts. The reasons cited included lost sales to competitors, customer-related delays in the construction of centers, and additional ProteusONE installation costs attributable to teething problems with the system. These issues arose amid uncertainty in the United States following the Trump administration's announcement of plans to reform Obamacare, and in China, which was reviewing its five-year plan.

Aside from internal delays, a second factor put pressure on IBA's profit margins: a fierce commercial war, especially with the American company Varian. Despite its size, Varian had not managed to challenge IBA's position as the global leader. Its proton therapy division experienced significant losses year after year. In third place, Hitachi proved to be a strong competitor, while Mevion concentrated on the compact systems segment.

Thirdly, some observers questioned the future of proton therapy and IBA's ability to successfully navigate an industry facing many external uncertainties. Several obstacles hindered the adoption of this technology. In contrast, the oncology pharmaceutical industry had developed a business model that enabled it to set and maintain high prices. It relied on randomized clinical trials to prove drug effectiveness and had a strong sales force and influential lobbying power to promote its products. Proton therapy providers, however, had to build evidence of their effectiveness after the fact through hospital feedback, which required sufficient facilities and patient volume. This process delayed and complicated establishing the clinical benefits of proton therapy. Insurance companies, especially in the United States, were often hesitant to reimburse these treatments, which, combined with a lack of awareness among referring physicians and concerns about financial losses for conventional radiotherapy centers, slowed the process of redirecting patients.

For the third time in its history, IBA's share price plummeted, reaffirming that companies like this should be evaluated based on long-term trends rather than quarterly results. A few more or fewer contracts during a specific period can significantly influence external perceptions, creating a disconnect between stock market performance and the company's actual health. By the end of 2017, market capitalization fell from €1.4 billion to €850 million, and by the end of 2018, it further declined to €525 million, with the negative trend continuing into the next financial year. However, this time, there was no need for existential doubt. Currently, IBA has sufficient resources and experience to withstand the storm and emerge stronger than ever.

EMBRACING TOMORROW

[2018-2026]

6

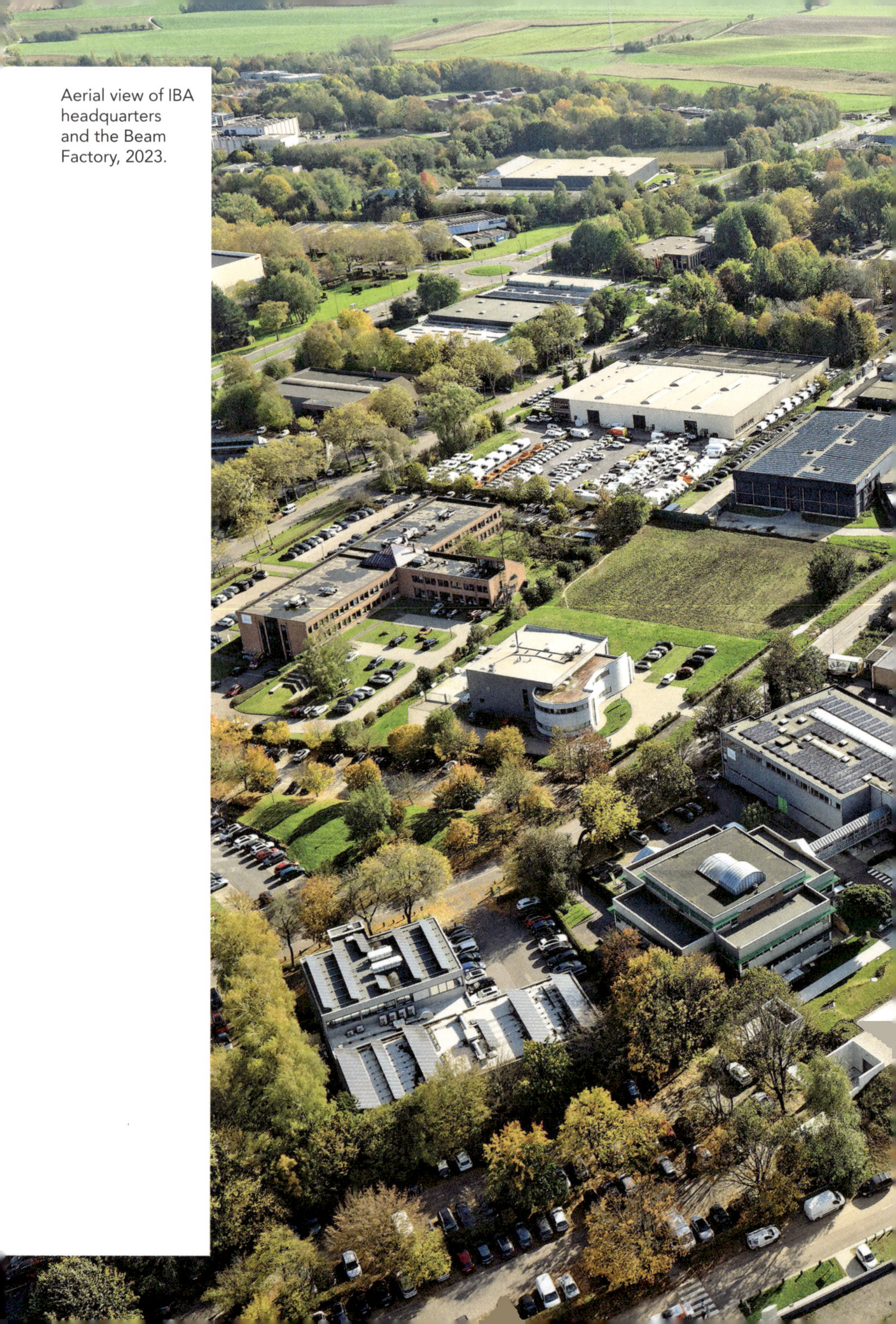

Aerial view of IBA headquarters and the Beam Factory, 2023.

Adapting to an upside-down world

Crises provided IBA with opportunities to streamline its organization, reallocate resources, and cut unnecessary expenses, all while maintaining its competitive and technological advantages. In 2017, facing challenges, IBA's management took a cautious approach, implementing furloughs to evaluate market trends before making more structural decisions.

Proton therapy was a key part of IBA's portfolio, with sector changes reflecting the company's luck. Although many projects were in progress worldwide, their completion and the finalization of customer financing were uncertain. Instead of relying on the strong growth seen in 2015 and 2016, IBA focused on a steady base with room for growth. The company reorganized its proton therapy business unit to improve efficiency, giving regional project managers a larger role in building customer facilities.

At the group level, IBA streamlined its hierarchical structure to enhance visibility and accountability. The company shifted its focus toward the Radiopharma and Industrial business units, which had previously been overshadowed by proton therapy and where new opportunities were emerging. IBA also conducted a study on the potential sale of its dosimetry business.

In early 2019, IBA launched the *RISE* project with McKinsey, aiming to reduce complexity, enhance resilience to market fluctuations, ensure product delivery during peak demand times, strengthen stakeholder engagement, and navigate increasingly complex regulations. About thirty employees were laid off—an uncommon event at IBA.

These adjustments restored profitability in 2019, boosted by a rebound in proton therapy sales. IBA remained the only profitable supplier in the market, despite margins being squeezed by fierce competition. On the other hand, accelerator sales grew considerably, and recurring services made up nearly 40 percent of revenue, thanks to the company's broad base of installed units.

The onset of the COVID-19 pandemic introduced new challenges. Disruptions to supply chains, travel restrictions, remote work, and impacts on healthcare systems complicated operations and made projects less predictable. Nonetheless, IBA's dedicated teams navigated this period with agility, collaborating through innovative goal-tracking methods. The company's digitalization allowed remote work, including predictive and corrective maintenance of systems. Some solutions proved essential during this unprecedented time, especially in meeting increased demand for medical sterilization. As IBA's activities were considered vital to the community, the company was less affected by construction stoppages and lockdowns than many others. Decentralized teams operating proton therapy centers continued their mission to support patient treatment without interruption.

In 2020, as the COVID-19 crisis devastated the global economy, IBA's signing of a major framework agreement in China boosted results and eased competitive pressures. China—and the broader Asia-Pacific region—became the center of growth for proton therapy. Given the large local population, centers needed systems with multiple treatment rooms. Instead of waiting for a government-backed Chinese competitor to emerge, IBA anticipated developments and signed a strategic licensing deal with CGN Nuclear Technology Application (CGNNT), worth over €100 million plus royalties on future sales. Under this agreement, IBA granted CGNNT an exclusive license for its original ProteusPLUS solution across mainland China, while retaining the option to finalize up to five contracts already under negotiation. The partnership involved transferring expertise, providing training, and offering technical support, but excluded the latest ProteusONE technology. After assessing the risks of technology transfer, IBA strategically partnered with a Chinese nuclear giant to seize a market poised for significant growth under the government's "Healthy China 2030" program. This move allowed IBA to put into practice its playful slogan: "Designed in Wallifornia, made in China".[43]

Building up

As the new decade began, over 550 IBA accelerators were in use worldwide, and the milestone of 100,000 patients treated with proton therapy had been achieved. Building on extensive experience from numerous entrepreneurial ventures over thirty-five years, IBA established itself as a leader in developing profitable business models centered on its particle accelerators. Although the company was organized into four business units—with dosimetry ultimately remaining within the group—many connections and synergies thrived among the different sectors. Each unit contributed to IBA's mission to protect, improve, and save lives in its own way. In both prosperous and challenging times, innovation has remained the company's foundation. This commitment is especially clear today as IBA celebrates its forty-year anniversary. Every day, 200 engineers work to improve IBA's technologies, which are protected by over 500 patents.

The Holy Grail of theranostics and alpha

In the 2010s, theranostics became a key milestone in advancing personalized medicine, raising the profile of nuclear medicine within the broader medical community. Theranostics relies on sequential use of a single targeting molecule: when combined with a gamma or positron-emitting isotope, it enables diagnosis via scintigraphy or PET imaging; when paired with a beta or alpha-emitting isotope, it functions as a therapeutic agent capable of selectively destroying tumor cells while reducing side effects. Although the idea was not entirely new —iodine-131 had long demonstrated this dual role in treating thyroid issues— theranostics truly gained momentum in the 2010s, thanks to progress in radiopharmacy. The most advanced approach in this area is alpha immunotherapy, which utilizes alpha emitters—powerful, precise helium nuclei—to target disease with remarkable accuracy.

PET imaging showing marked regression of advanced prostate cancer after experimental targeted treatment with actinium-225.

PanTera plant project for the production of actinium-225, 2024.

For IBA, this emerging dual field presented an opportunity to further elevate its mission. The company's accelerators enabled physicians to reliably produce a wide range of rare radioisotopes and turn theranostics and targeted alpha therapies into practical realities. Pioneering research started in 2008 at the Arronax center in Nantes, where the Cyclone 70 multiparticle accelerator was used to produce the alpha emitter astatine-211. The Cyclone 30XP was also built for this purpose, while the Cyclone IKON—successor to the renowned Cyclone 30—produces various radioisotopes, including gallium-68 and copper-64 for theranostic uses.

Equally notable, a joint effort between IBA's Radiopharma and Industrial business units led Rhodotron experts to realize that electron accelerators could also be used to produce vital radioisotopes.

Initially, IBA partnered with Northstar, a U.S. company, to develop a new Rhodotron, the TT300-HE, offering an environmentally friendly solution to the looming shortage of molybdenum-99—a vital isotope traditionally produced in nuclear reactors with an uncertain future. Molybdenum-99 is the primary precursor to technetium-99m, which is used in 80 percent of SPECT diagnostic imaging procedures in oncology and cardiology. The first machine, tested in the Louvain-la-Neuve bunker, was shipped to Northstar's Wisconsin plant in 2020, followed by four more for increasingly varied applications. Further discoveries showed that these same Rhodotrons could also generate new therapeutic radioisotopes, such as copper-67 and actinium-225—another alpha emitter—both of which can be used in theranostics. Actinium-225, in particular, has the potential to target and destroy cancer cells with unprecedented precision across many cancer types, including metastases throughout the body.

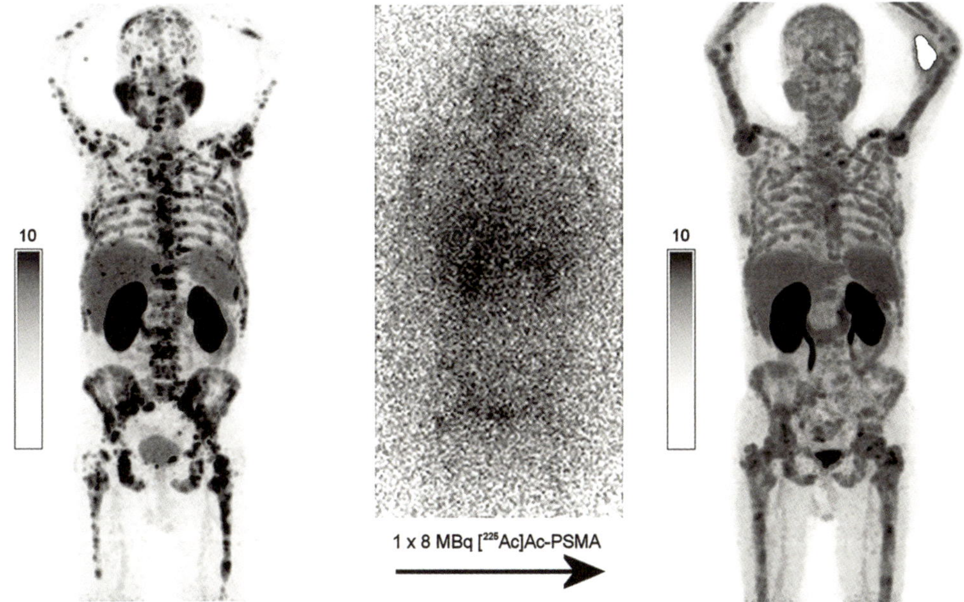
10
10
1 x 8 MBq [225Ac]Ac-PSMA
PSA = 727 ng/mL
PSA = 342 ng/mL

Buoyed by this initial breakthrough, IBA entered into a research and development partnership in 2021 with SCK-CEN, a leading European producer of radioisotopes from the Mol nuclear reactor in Belgium. Rather than simply selling its accelerators, IBA aimed to invest in growing the business to capture more value. The following year, the two partners established the PanTera joint venture to produce large quantities of actinium-225, leveraging SCK-CEN's exceptional stock of radium—an inheritance from Belgian mining operations in Congo. PanTera soon partnered with the American green-tech company TerraPower Isotopes, founded by Bill Gates and others, to speed up small-scale production of actinium-225 and help pharmaceutical companies like Novartis and Bayer advance their clinical development. In 2024, PanTera signed an agreement with Bayer to ensure its supply. That same year, a successful fundraising campaign brought the value of PanTera to €280 million—highlighting the medical community's high expectations for this radioisotope.

Using similar logic, IBA formed an alliance in 2025 with France's Framatome to develop a network of cyclotrons for producing astatine-211 in Europe and the United States. Through these strategic partnerships, IBA once again pursued a downstream diversification strategy. This time, however, the approach was more cautious—completely dependent on collaborations and less capital-intensive.

The age of X-Rays

Very early on—perhaps too early—IBA believed in the transformative potential of electron beams and X-rays for sterilization. As a pioneer in this technology since the 1990s, following the development of the Rhodotron and later the Rhodotron Duo launched in 2014, the company ultimately had to wait a quarter of a century before this traditionally conservative sector began to genuinely adopt these innovations.

Starting in 2018, under Thomas Servais's leadership, the Industrial business unit gained new momentum. The previous opportunistic and somewhat fragmented commercial approach was replaced by a focus on a select number of promising applications, especially in medical sterilization. The team was reorganized, and several unprofitable product lines—particularly in the Dynamitron segment—were discontinued, allowing IBA to refocus on services and upgrades. A new, improved version of the Rhodotron was launched, featuring pulsed technology that used less electricity, offered greater modularity, and had increased energy capacity. The integrated approach was further developed, enabling Industrial to provide customers with highly automated, turnkey solutions. These included assistance with building design, accelerator configuration, safety, dosimetry, control systems, conveyors, automated pallet handling, support, and training—anywhere in the world.

As with proton therapy, IBA aimed to change attitudes and methods by educating political and economic decision-makers about the technical and health benefits of electron and X-ray irradiation compared to older techniques. To support this effort, a user experience and training center—Indux—was opened in Louvain-la-Neuve, and a research center—Feerix—was established with partner Aerial in Strasbourg to familiarize the professional sterilization community with the latest techniques.

All these efforts were crowned with success tenfold during the Covid-19 crisis, which caused demand for medical sterilization solutions to soar across Europe, America, and Asia. Sales skyrocketed before returning to normal, fueled by excess capacity at the height of the health crisis. Still, the momentum had been set in motion. The shift to X-ray sterilization was finally happening. By trusting in it and staying committed, IBA established itself as the leading supplier.

Building on this renewed momentum, Industrial began exploring entirely new technologies in food irradiation and environmental applications, such

The Feerix experimental irradiation platform set up with Aerial in Strasbourg, France, 2019.

as wastewater treatment and PFAS decontamination—the so-called "forever chemicals" now widespread in the environment. Combined with the new use of Rhodotrons for radioisotope production and the long-awaited enthusiasm for X-rays, this business unit, once in decline, was now starting to emerge as a strong growth driver for IBA.

Proton therapy: precision, speed, adaptability, and Hope for All

The fresh opportunity created by the framework agreement with CGNNT in China allowed IBA to stick to its ambitious innovation and development plan.

Determined to leverage its key strength—unmatched execution capabilities—IBA set itself apart by providing the fastest installation times in the industry and notably high equipment uptime. For hospitals and patients alike, this meant investments that quickly yielded tangible treatments and maximum system availability.

The company aimed to streamline its offerings around a single platform, designed for easy deployment and maintenance, while integrating three key and differentiating features: adaptive treatment, arc therapy, and Flash.

Adaptive treatment continuously considers doses already administered, changes in the organs being treated, and patient movement, thereby enhancing accuracy. Arc therapy employs a continuously rotating beam around the patient, reducing treatment time by up to 35 percent and improving dose conformity. This innovation, supported by a public subsidy from the Walloon cluster MecaTech, was developed in partnership with the Beaumont Therapy Center in Michigan, where initial testing began in 2023.

IBA cooperates with the Beaumont Proton Therapy Center in Michigan to develop arc therapy technology, 2017.

Pushing boundaries further, Flash therapy investigates the possibility of delivering treatment at ultra-high speeds, in just a fraction of a second. Once clinically validated, this approach could revolutionize the economic model of proton therapy, boosting equipment capacity thirtyfold while reducing the cost per treatment. The initial experiments began with the universities of Pennsylvania, Reading in the United Kingdom, and Groningen in the Netherlands starting in 2018.

Meanwhile, IBA invested in training and sharing best practices. In 2021, it launched the first online proton therapy platform—Campus—that unites clinicians, researchers, and engineers in a collaborative, educational setting. This platform creates a global community vital for speeding up the clinical development of proton therapy and increasing its adoption.

These developments occurred in a rapidly evolving market. In 2022, after being acquired by Siemens Healthineers, Varian announced it would stop selling new proton therapy systems due to unprofitability. Although this decision temporarily cast doubt on proton therapy's reputation, it eased competitive pressure and clearly reaffirmed IBA's leadership. Successes in sales soon followed. In 2022, IBA achieved a record of 17 rooms sold in a single year, including 10 in a market of unprecedented size with the Spanish Ministry of Health.

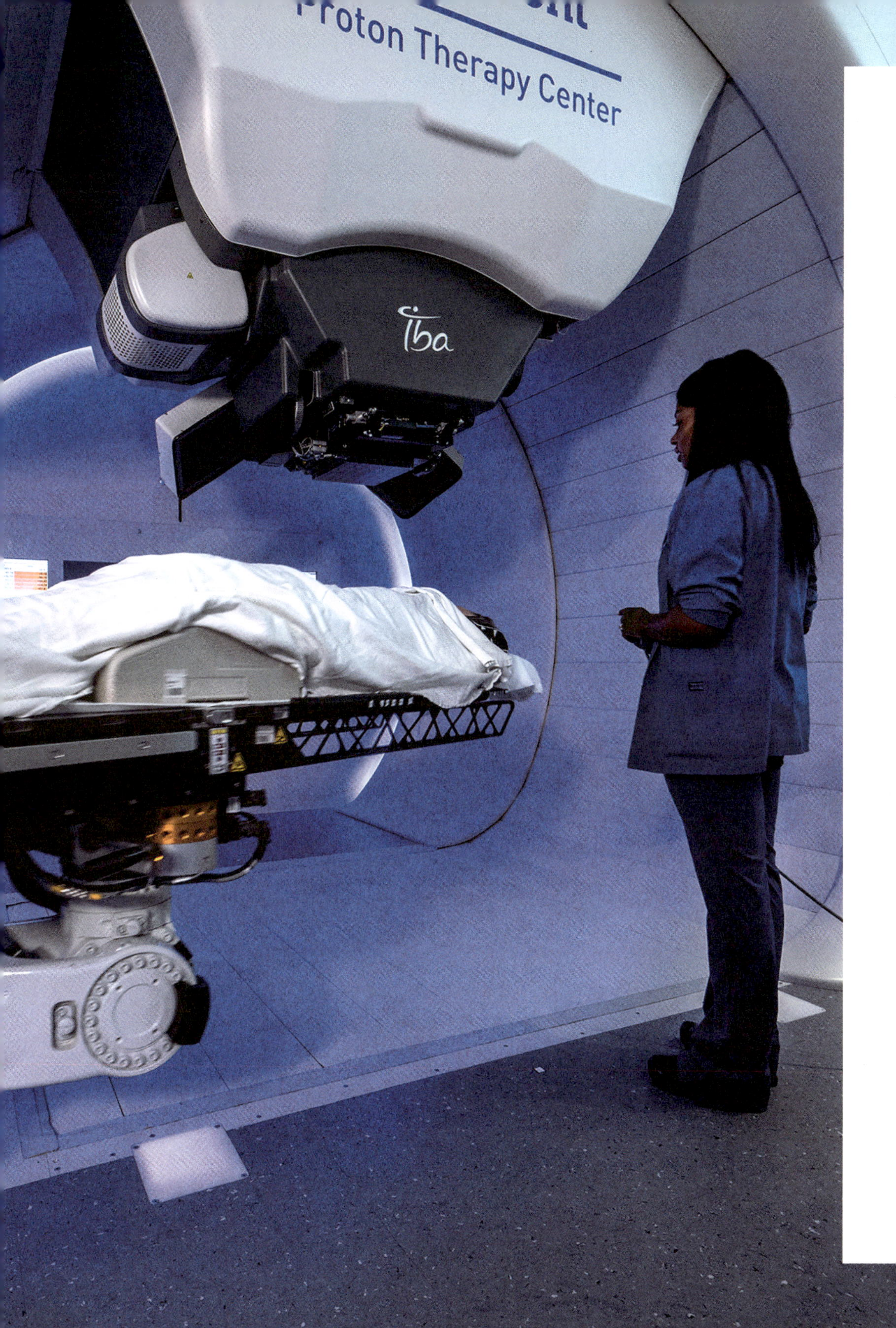
Proton Therapy Center
iba

Alongside advances in proton therapy, since 2008, IBA has maintained a long-term partnership with various public and private partners in the Normandy region focused on hadron therapy. This technique, which uses heavy carbon ions to treat radiation-resistant tumors, largely remained unused due to its high cost and complexity. It wasn't until the technical, financial, and institutional conditions aligned in 2019 that the project moved forward, with the formal creation of a joint venture—Normandy Hadrontherapy (NHa)—and the announced completion of the large C400 multi-ion cyclotron, scheduled for 2027. This once again highlights IBA's dedication to paving the way in particle therapy.

By combining a streamlined platform, breakthrough innovations like Arc and Flash, an active community with Campus, recognized operational efficiency, and support for research into emerging technologies, IBA continues to establish itself as the undisputed global leader in proton therapy, in a market where competition struggles and medical demand continues to grow. The fight for profitability is to be won inch by inch.

When sustainability rhymes with longevity

IBA's commitment to sustainability and stakeholder harmony has steadily grown, driven by both core beliefs and strategic planning. Having reached a point of stability, the company aimed to increase its positive impact while protecting its long-term future.

In 2018, this vision found a concrete application with the construction of the Beam Factory in Louvain-la-Neuve. This highly energy-efficient building combined superior insulation, extensive use of natural light, renewable energy sources, and heat recovery from accelerator testing, meeting 95 percent of its heating and cooling demands. The use of innovative materials, like low-activation concrete—which ultimately reduces the amount of radioactive waste needing reprocessing—demonstrates the company's commitment to long-term sustainability.

IBA's leaders drew inspiration from visionary figures like Jacques Crahay, Emmanuel Faber, Bertrand Piccard, Yvon Chouinard, and Ray Anderson. Their openness led them to discover the B Corp model, created in the United States in 2006 to redefine business purpose as a force for good. "B Corp is the benchmark that we forgot to invent but have been living by for thirty years", summarized Olivier Legrain.[44] Certification became an obvious choice, allowing the company to formalize long-standing commitments and develop a plan for ongoing improvement.

To ensure alignment between governance and mission, IBA took several decisive steps. In 2018, a sustainability committee was established within the Board of Directors. In 2020, the company's articles of incorporation were amended to explicitly include the goal of having a positive impact on all

To.
Infinity
And
Beyond

The five-pointed star symbolizes the balance that IBA constantly strives to achieve between its stakeholders.

The Beam Factory in Louvain-la-Neuve, focused on eco-friendly building design, 2019.

stakeholders, "while respecting life and future generations". That same year, IBA utilized a new legal provision to introduce double voting rights for long-term shareholders, thereby strengthening the project's stability in the face of speculation. Since 2021, sustainability has been the responsibility of the entire Board, with each director accountable for these issues.

Social responsibility also showed in the company's compensation policy. In 2021, IBA introduced a profit-sharing plan to connect the interests of employees and shareholders. When a dividend was paid, it triggered a profit-sharing scheme of similar value, adjusted based on responsibility levels.

After two years of preparation, IBA achieved B Corp certification in 2021, joining the exclusive group of certified listed companies. The rating system is based on two pillars: the impact of the business model and operational impact. With its mission embedded in its articles of association, IBA scored highly in the first category. Areas for improvement were mainly identified in the second category, especially regarding the environment and community relations.

This assessment led to the creation of a roadmap focused on six strategic priorities: designing products with low carbon footprints and minimal waste; cutting by half Scope 1 and 2 emissions by 2030; reducing unsorted waste by two-thirds by 2025; developing a sustainable supply chain by encouraging suppliers to improve their impact; promoting a diverse, equitable, and inclusive workplace; and ultimately, enhancing transparency, mission, and accountability across all company practices.

No fewer than forty-five projects were launched across these six areas, including eco-design, digital transformation, reverse logistics, improving product energy efficiency, use of renewable energy, soft mobility, setting an internal carbon price, contributing to decarbonization through sustainable agriculture projects, packaging and recycling, inclusion through collective intelligence processes, sustainability training, collaborations with suppliers, and external outreach. To ensure consistency, 34 percent of managers' variable compensation was directly linked to B Corp results.

Results followed. In 2024, IBA achieved recertification with a score of 114 points, up from 90 previously, thanks largely to operational improvements. The company ranked in the top 10 percent of the 9,300 certified companies and in the top 5 percent of the 146 companies with more than 1,000 employees. This collective momentum confirmed that IBA's commitment to sustainability was not just one project among many, but an inexorable driving force.

For IBA, sustainability encompasses not only environmental and social factors but also its time aspect: how can the company's independence and mission be maintained over the long term? Since the hostile takeover attempt in 1996, this question has stayed central for the founders and their successors.

Since 1997, Belgian Anchorage has served as a major shareholder, protecting IBA from potential hostile takeovers. Several initiatives have been undertaken to strengthen this entrepreneurial foundation. In 2020, the company was renamed Sustainable Anchorage. It held approximately 20 percent of the capital, and 30 percent of the voting rights. Its articles of association are aligned with IBA's social mission, stipulating that its investments must have a positive impact on all stakeholders, "respecting life and present and future generations, and minimizing any negative environmental and social impacts".

Meanwhile, an investment vehicle called Management Anchorage was established in 2020 to assist IBA executives in securing generational succession. This transition concluded in December 2024 when several heirs of the original shareholders expressed their desire to divest. Management Anchorage acquired 21 percent of Sustainable Anchorage through a deal involving the sale of IBA's shares and financing spread over ten years. This move opened up the capital to about fifty managers and employees—the "entrepreneurs of the future"—providing them with direct representation within the main shareholding structure. It strengthened both IBA's stability and the commitment of the younger generations to its governance.

By the end of 2025, the shareholding structure was as follows: Sustainable Anchorage held 30.5 percent of voting rights, other long-standing shareholders and allies held 16.7 percent, banks and institutional investors held 21.2 percent, and the public held 31.6 percent. This distribution reflects IBA's history—a company rooted in its community and open to the world, aiming to stabilize its shareholding structure in line with its values.

From an operational standpoint, the company has been re-evaluating its organization and culture to support growth while remaining true to its core values.

In 2023, IBA welcomed Henri de Romrée, a former McKinsey partner and BPost executive. Appointed Chief Strategy Officer and later Deputy CEO, he was responsible for exploring new growth opportunities, improving the organization, and boosting the performance of the rapidly expanding Industrial and Radio-pharma business units. He also temporarily served as Chief Financial Officer before Catherine Vandenborre, formerly of the Elia Group, joined the company in 2025.

In 2024, an in-depth analysis brought all employees together around a single question: what kind of organization would allow us to dream bigger? The solution was to create two more homogeneous entities; each focused on executing and developing their activities while maintaining overall consistency. This vision translated into a three-pronged structure: the clinical entity, encompassing proton therapy and dosimetry with 1,300 employees; the technology entity, dedicated to nuclear medicine and sterilization with 550 employees; and the

B Corp certification ceremony at the Brussels Stock Exchange, 2021.

The company's mobility policy aims to limit environmental impact, 2023.

corporate unit, a 170-member team responsible for ensuring the group's operations and exploring new sources of value creation. This unit included the Discovery Lab; an open innovation laboratory and incubator focused on emerging applications. This hybrid model, combining greater autonomy for individual entities with overall strategic alignment, aimed to improve agility, decision-making speed, and efficiency. Olivier Legrain remained CEO while directly supervising proton therapy, a sector so strategic that it required his personal involvement.

Meanwhile, a change in working methods and behaviors was encouraged. During the 2020 health crisis, executives began reflecting on the future of IBA and concluded that the next cultural evolution would involve harnessing collective intelligence. This vision led to the 'At our Best' program, which breaks with management based on individual annual targets. The program promotes collective value creation through continuous feedback, coaching, the OKR (Objectives and Key Results) method, and ongoing dialogue that allows the organization to "take its pulse". Management styles shifted toward greater humility, collaboration, and trust, supported by networks of internal coaches and facilitators specializing in collective and emotional intelligence. The compensation policy embodied this philosophy: fixed salaries rewarded skills, while variable pay was now primarily based on collective performance, thanks to a profit-sharing plan equivalent to the dividends paid to shareholders.

By reshaping its organization and changing its culture, IBA has acquired the tools necessary to grow, fulfill its goals, and keep integrating innovation, performance, and shared responsibility, in line with its original philosophy.

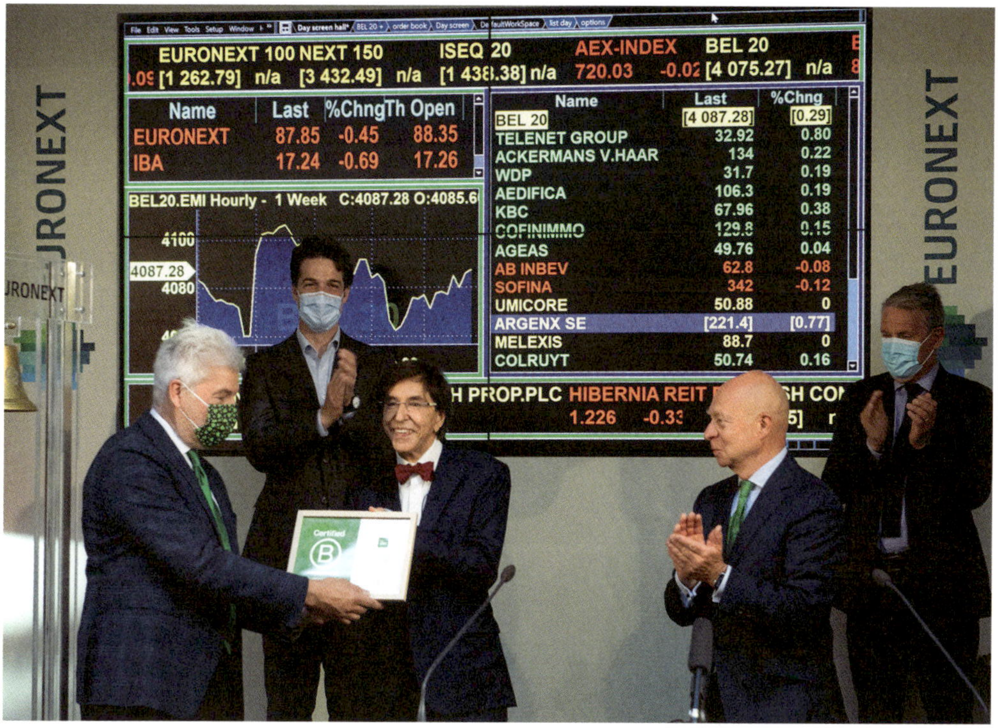
EURONEXT 100 NEXT 150
ISEQ 20
AEX-INDEX
BEL 20
[1 262.79] n/a [3 432.49] n/a
720.03
[4 075.27] n/a
Name Last %ChngTh Open
EURONEXT 87.85 -0.45 88.35
IBA 17.24 -0.69 17.26
BEL20.EMI Hourly - 1 Week C:4087.28 O:4085.6
4100
4087.28
4080
Name Last %Chng
BEL 20 [4 087.28] [0.29]
TELENET GROUP 32.92 0.80
ACKERMANS V.HAAR 134 0.22
WDP 31.7 0.19
AEDIFICA 106.3 0.19
KBC 67.96 0.38
COFINIMMO 129.8 0.15
AGEAS 49.76 0.04
AB INBEV 62.8 -0.08
SOFINA 342 -0.12
UMICORE 50.88 0
ARGENX SE [221.4] [0.77]
MELEXIS 88.7 0
COLRUYT 50.74 0.16
HIBERNIA REIT
1.226
EURONEXT
Certified

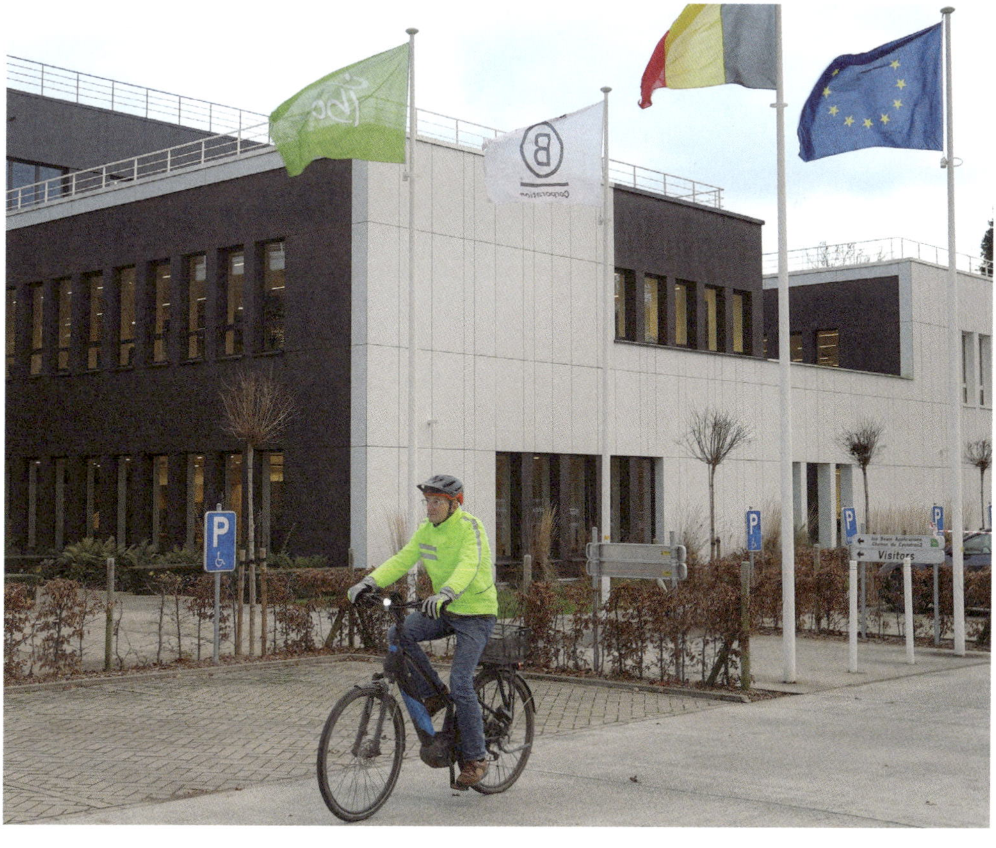
P
Visitors

RESTLESS INNOVATORS, ARTISANS OF HOPE: THE IBA PHILOSOPHY

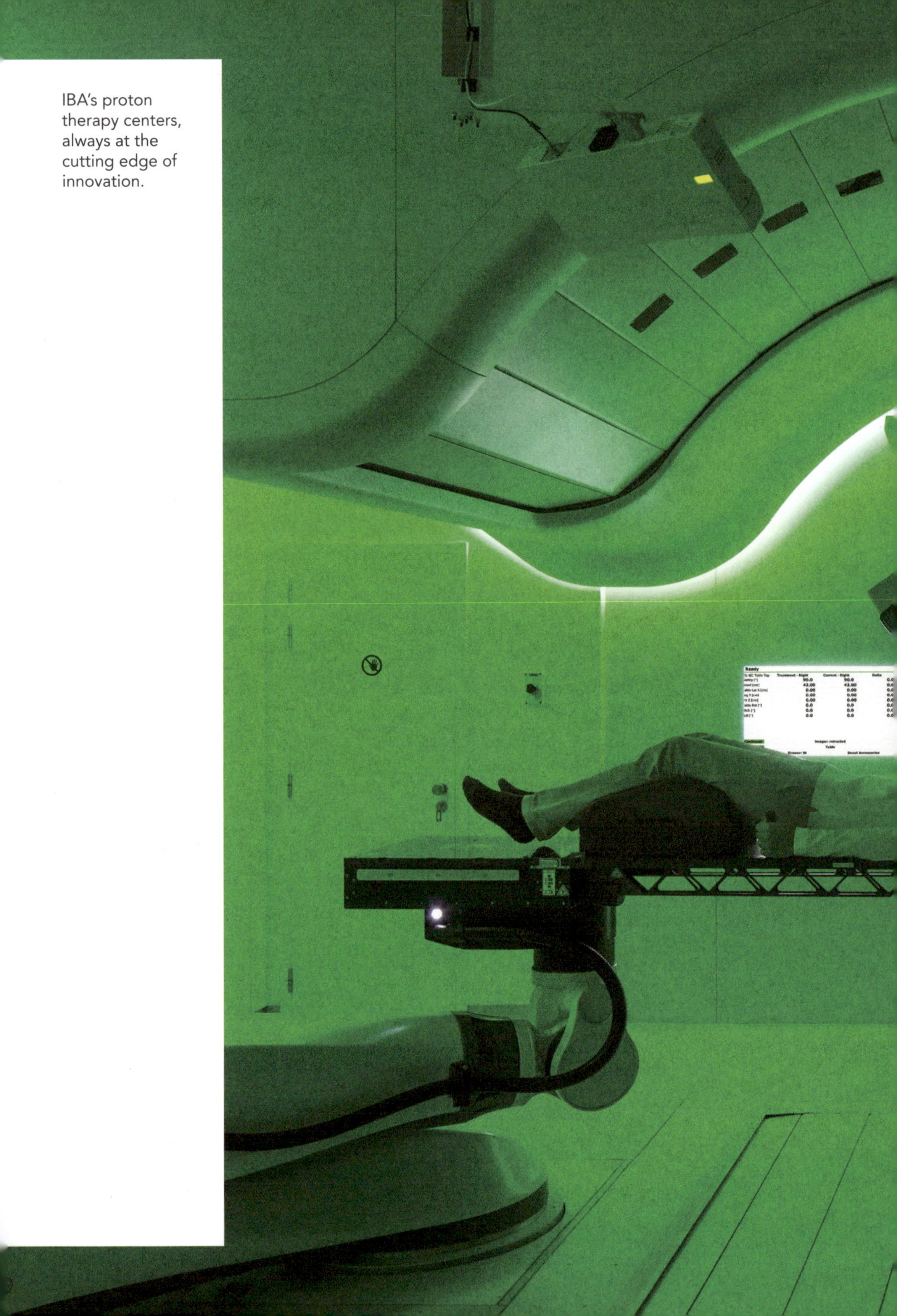

IBA's proton therapy centers, always at the cutting edge of innovation.

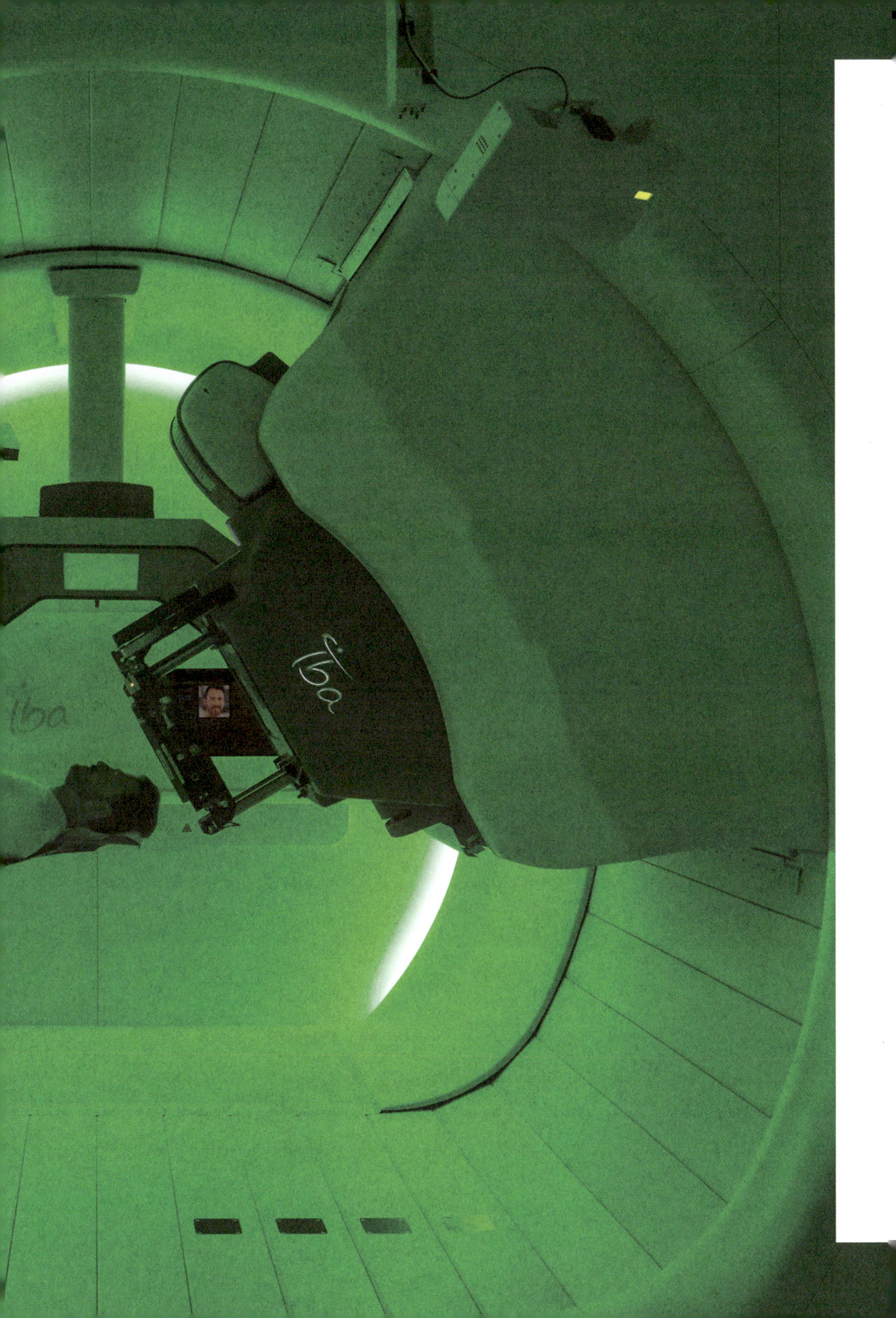

FOUNDING PRINCIPLES

1

Pierre Mottet,
Olivier Legrain,
and Yves Jongen,
2016.

Entrepreneurship, Innovation, and Responsibility

The first chairman of the IBA board, Philippe de Woot, had a lasting influence on the spirit that guides the company's leaders in all their decisions. He described the entrepreneur with three qualities: a vision of possible progress, the courage to implement it, and the power of conviction capable of securing the necessary support and resources. The economist Schumpeter demonstrated that, through creativity, the entrepreneurial innovator transforms competition via "creative destruction" and, in pursuit of profit, opens the way to new models. De Woot emphasized that the company—as a "collective entrepreneur"—amplifies these qualities: a shared vision drives the organization forward, courage translates into bold decisions, and conviction facilitates the dissemination of innovation.

However, he warned that the ability to innovate is never guaranteed; it depends on talented individuals or teams working within a culture that encourages disruption and change. This is one of the main challenges facing companies, as their size often leads to bureaucracy, inertia, and resistance to change. "Innovation cannot be entirely programmed. It is a state of mind, momentum, life, and movement. It involves an intertwining of vision, energy, intuition, and trial and error. It fluctuates, hesitates, recovers, and pushes forward. It cannot be codified and is constantly renewing itself. It largely resists analysis and models. This means the innovation process is fragile and only thrives when the internal and external environments are sufficiently favorable".[45]

Philippe de Woot also noted that, with the global rise of innovation-driven technosciences, companies have gained more power, which creates opportunities but also risks when their purpose is solely focused on economic performance. He therefore argued that companies should expand their role: to promote the common good, adopt a future-oriented ethic, and take on shared responsibility at the global level.

The history of IBA illustrates this tension between innovation and responsibility. Its ability to develop a competitive technological advantage, to unite a community over time, to serve science, health, and the common good, and to adapt to changing circumstances are core principles promoted by Philippe de Woot. This management philosophy, strengthened over the years, continues to build its future and lead by example.

An alternative innovator-entrepreneur

Yves Jongen exemplifies the qualities of an innovator-entrepreneur, acting as a catalyst for industry transformation by launching a groundbreaking new product. In 1986, he and his team redesigned the industrial cyclotron in less than a year. By axially injecting the negative-ion source from outside, utilizing stripping extraction, and rethinking the magnet design and radio-frequency system, they created a machine that was five times more powerful, three times more economical, and immediately outpaced competitors. When introduced, the Cyclone 30 was a disruptive innovation that changed the field and forced competitors to adapt or become obsolete.

Yet, the purpose he defined for his company at its founding was not exactly the entrepreneurial profit described by Schumpeter. Although he came from a wealthy family, Yves was motivated by progressive ideas. His main ambition was not to become rich or to sell his start-up to a large company to become a "man of means". He dreamed of a long-lasting industrial company that would serve as a social model, offering quality jobs to young graduates in his region and inspiring Wallonia, which struggled with industrial restructuring and where entrepreneurship had fallen out of favor. He also felt a moral duty to give back to the socioeconomic environment that had enabled his success.

Having frequently debated the social organization of the company with his unionist and anarchist friends, he concluded that the old theory of class struggle supported by certain unions was outdated and archaic. Similarly, he viewed the positions of the business world as generally timid and self-interested, lacking a broad and modern outlook.

As he writes: "I believe that a business is like a ship caught in a storm. To survive, the captain, officers, and crew must all work together as a team in the face of external danger. They must realize that they will either survive together or sink together, and that their unity matters far more than their differences. When I look at a social conflict, I am often struck by the lack of openness, intelligence, and vision on both sides, and I think that it should be possible to do much better".[46]

Rebellious? Utopian? Alternative? Regardless of the label, the initial goal was genuine: gather about fifteen scientists and technicians to generate enough revenue to sustain innovation collaboratively, mainly for the joy of it, and to advance particle engineering for medicine and patients. "IBA is a group of people working together on a great project": this statement has stayed true in its heartfelt candor, providing a striking contrast to the technical solutions developed.

Close collaboration between IBA team members and a Japanese client's team on Christmas Eve, 1990.

Mobilizing talent

Idealism does not equal weakness or frivolity. The pioneers of IBA worked tirelessly, often on Saturdays and Sundays, including evenings. "I often asked too much of those who worked alongside me with extraordinary loyalty and dedication", admits Yves. As for Pierre, no one ever knew where he was, but his messages arrived at all hours and days of the week, whether he was in Belgium or Tokyo. The initial technical team consisted of about twenty experts: electromechanical engineers, automation engineers, physicists, and specialists in radio frequency, vacuum, and power electronics. Together, they ranked among the best in the world in their fields and, united behind a shared vision, formed the core of IBA's innovation. They were motivated by the nearly insurmountable technical challenges they faced.

When IBA decided early on to diversify its product line to spread its risks, the team was encouraged to achieve "a small miracle every day": the simultaneous development of three new, unfunded cyclotron models, the six-month development of targets and chemical synthesizers for Erasmus Hospital, super-powerful and compact cyclotrons for brachytherapy, the industrialization of the Rhodotron, not to mention the bold effort to enter the still-nonexistent commercial proton therapy market against the largest technology companies on the planet, on their own turf. These achievements were reached with great scientific rigor, but without any truly standardized procedures other than "quality, deadline, and cost"[47], based on a rough strategy, calculations jotted down on the back of an envelope, and brilliant intuitions... which sometimes led to serious financial consequences. However, these highly ambitious decisions taken in the first five or six years laid the technological foundation for the company for decades to come. From that point onward, IBA established itself as a small technology holding company ready to deploy its innovative solutions in high-value applications. Some of these were not pursued internally but were spun off into separate companies, such as microfiltration membranes (IT4IP with Roger Legras) and engine component wear testing (IDS with Thierry Delvigne), thereby contributing to a positive indirect impact. The experience then inspired employees to venture out on their own, such as Jean-Luc Morelle (Coincidence and Trasis) and Antoine Pouppez (NeuroClues).

A second key factor in stabilizing and even ensuring the company's survival was the successful recruitment of Pierre Mottet in 1988. This brilliant university student, a disciple of Philippe de Woot, strategist, and "chess player who anticipates several moves ahead", belongs to the school of strategic planning: "Not for forecasts, which will inevitably be wrong, but for exploring possible paths and the best way to prepare for them", he explains. Like a guardian angel, he made sure that things happened. He balanced Yves's dynamic personality, a fan of absolute agility. When Yves stated, "It's better to be first than to be better", Pierre countered with, "It's better to be better than to be first."

The two friends frequently explored the countryside of Louvain-la-Neuve, trying to persuade each other of the best way to reach a goal, while generally agreeing on the outcome. They faced different risks and negotiated accordingly: Yves minimized the technical difficulties to sell his machine, while Pierre was mainly focused on pricing it high enough to keep the company running. "I was hired to sell. Yves and I were not equals, but he was willing to surround himself with people more skilled than he in various areas, letting everyone find their role. We quickly divided the responsibilities: he handled the technical side, and I managed everything else.", he explains. The goal was to avoid a common trap for university spin-offs: academic researchers often aren't suited to run a business, and when they are forced to work with a financier who stifles their creativity, the company can lose direction. For many colleagues who observed the chemistry between the two managers, Pierre's biggest achievement was guiding Yves's energy without killing his enthusiasm. Yves, who always wanted to stay close to the workshop, believes that passing the CEO role to Pierre was one of the best decisions of his life.

Although their methods differed, both men shared the same view of the role of business in society. Yves repeatedly affirmed his desire to "leave the world in a better state than he found it". Pierre shared a similar perspective, though with a slightly different emphasis. Both were inspired by Philippe de Woot's teachings on corporate social responsibility and, more generally, by an academic philosophy that goes beyond just material concerns: "In the early meetings, we would mostly talk about customers, organization, and social ambition. Then Éric de Lamotte joined us to oversee the finances and rebalance the approach", Pierre notes.

The arrival of Éric de Lamotte, a disciplined financier, strengthened the management team, transforming it into a triumvirate without diminishing their enthusiasm. Breaking the norms of "managerial correctness" fostered a healthy imbalance. A friendly and trusting relationship developed among the three leaders, making their discussions even more passionate.

– Éric: "… Why should I follow the advice of a man who was responsible for the worst financial disaster in IBA's history?"

– Yves: "Éric, never having done anything in your life is an advantage, but you shouldn't overplay it."

– Pierre: "Gentlemen, I leave you for two days, and when I return, you've started your own Kosovo war…"

This story highlights a culture of open, honest, lively conversation, free of pretense and often infused with a touch of Belgian humor. There was a genuine sense of camaraderie within the SME, across all levels: "IBA was like a big family, very pleasant. I had lots of fun there. Yves and Pierre succeeded in recruiting fun and kind people. When they came back from a training course in England, they gave me a poster for my office: 'Wonder Woman works here'", says Anne-Marie Vranckx, senior executive assistant.

Before going public, transparency and information sharing were standard practice. Yves and Pierre started weekly staff meetings on Monday mornings, where everyone could openly discuss company news, including financial details and the progress of ongoing negotiations. This built a strong sense of unity

IBA

IBA staff gathering at the Louvain-la-Neuve offices to celebrate the company's tenth anniversary, 1996.

Celebration with the team from Japanese client Nihon Medi-Physics in the assembly hall at Pégard in Andenne, Belgium, 1990.

Preparing bids in the analog era took up a lot of space!

Every time a contract was signed or a project completed, the IBA team celebrated, here in 1998.

among the team. One question raised was: "How many months can we keep going with the money in the bank?" … "If it's more than six months, we'll be fine!" Before generating recurring revenue, IBA relied solely on current orders, creating a sense of urgency and constant watchfulness. However, thanks to its vision and expertise, it proved to be remarkably resilient: "We always think a company is fragile, but it is extremely resilient in the final moments, which allows it to bounce back", summarizes Pierre.

Full disclosure of information has never been harmful. On the contrary, it has allowed everyone to make well-informed decisions that helped them reach their goals. Transparency is also key with external parties, where possible. Before establishing IBA, Yves was preparing to present his cyclotron design at an international conference, even though it had not yet been patented! Since then, the experts at IBA have been quite open in sharing their advancements at scientific conferences: "We want to share our knowledge with society. This is our definition of sharing. We are part of larger ecosystems; we are involved. It's natural to let others benefit from it to increase its impact, and with an open policy, we sometimes receive more than we give. When we present at a conference to explain our progress, our competitors learn a little, but when we step down, people come to share their own experiences with us, which is also beneficial".[48] Obviously, this openness does not come at the expense of protecting inventions, as shown by the more than 500 patents filed since the company's founding and the maintenance of secrecy around vital know-how.

Ahead of its time, IBA developed a participatory management model inspired by university general assemblies, serving as a foundation for modern collective intelligence approaches. An internal memo from 1991 describes its philosophy: "In creating IBA, we wanted a company where everyone feels like part of a team working toward the same goal (…), where everyone has a say in organizing the company and their department (…), where people are happy to go to work every morning (…), and where, every time one of our cyclotrons leaves the factory to be installed elsewhere in the world, everyone feels pride in the result, telling themselves: 'That cyclotron is partly my work, either because I worked on it directly or because my work made it possible'".[49]

While many small businesses slowed their growth to avoid the legal threshold that would require social elections, Yves and Pierre always saw employee involvement in management as a source of strength. In 1989, well before it became a legal requirement, they naturally proposed holding informal early elections to send two employee representatives to the weekly management committee. Their contribution was seen as highly valuable, supporting the idea that giving employees a voice strengthens the company. Likewise, in 1987, employee and director share ownership was introduced so everyone could become an owner of "their" company and share in the rewards of collective effort, even though no dividends would be paid until 1997.

Employee empowerment was significantly boosted through accountability and resourcefulness. Field engineers, intervention technicians, and project managers were quickly thrown into challenging situations without much formal training. Some young graduates found themselves on the other side of the world, adjusting a beam on a machine worth several million euros in the dead of night and without any assistance. Helpfulness and sharing experience replaced formal procedures. The sense of belonging was reinforced by attaching the names of the design and assembly team members to a plaque on the machines, in a style similar to that used by artists. Some of the first sales representatives had to sell a cyclotron concept that didn't yet exist, set up exhibition booths at trade fairs, and clear customs for crates of equipment at airports. Project managers took responsibility for the entire process: purchasing parts, managing suppliers, ordering drawings, supervising engineering, and negotiating with customers. As several of them said: "At IBA, you're thrown against a steep cliff. Either you hang on and climb up, or you fall." Some become hooked, while others become discouraged. But everyone gains invaluable learning experience. As Yves explains: "IBA's greatest strength is its teams. Technologies can become obsolete, but having skilled team members who are able to adapt promotes longevity."

Furthermore, although the business venture started in the supportive environment of the University of Louvain-la-Neuve within a local ecosystem, IBA has consistently maintained a strong international identity. Because of its nature, the Cyclotron Research Center was mostly open to collaboration with other countries, supporting the development of science without borders. International conferences provided platforms where specialists shared their latest discoveries. The niche market for medical cyclotrons, limited to four systems each year, was inherently global: both tenders and technology monitoring extended far beyond national borders. IBA's earliest contracts reached across continents, extending to the United States, Australia, China, Japan, and even Iran. The company began operating in China before most Western firms, thanks to Frank Uyterhaegen, who had deep knowledge of the country's cultural dimensions. The IBA team traveled worldwide, often spending months away from their offices and families, adding an element of exoticism to their mission. The original IBA culture was thus open, optimistic, informal, empowering, international, and somewhat rebellious, while rooted in the region it aimed to support.

"What is admirable
in the history of IBA
is the genius
in action,
made possible
by a unique way
of managing people."

- Henri de Romrée

Principles vs. reality

Doubts forging character

While launching a start-up is exciting, it quickly faces existential questions that need practical solutions. This is especially true for the ongoing search for new funding sources to support program development.

IBA's first real-life test occurred in two rounds of restructuring in 1993 and 1994, following several years of losses and resulting in widespread layoffs. The question was: "How far can we amputate the leg without killing the patient?" During the works council meeting held the day after the announcement, the union representative interrupted the prepared presentation: "There's no need to convince us. We know that IBA's survival depends on restructuring. Tell us how many jobs have to be cut." When Yves replied "26", the representative agreed: "We had calculated 28. We accept 26. Now let's discuss the social criteria for deciding who will leave." Discussions continued into the night, ultimately leading to an agreement rarely seen in Belgium: a collective plan approved in a single meeting, without conflict. The following day, the management team met with the impacted employees, believing that transparency and dialogue would make this difficult time more humane and fairer.[50] During the second restructuring, the union representatives who had invited themselves to the talks were actually turned away by the staff. Since then, IBA has never experienced any labor disputes or strikes.

A second pivotal moment happened in 1996 when Canadian competitor MDS Nordion launched a hostile takeover attempt to acquire certain technologies before pulling the plug. An employee leveraged buyout seemed like the obvious solution. It was quickly carried out by most employees and directors, who believed in the company's future. Through a smart arrangement, Pierre Mottet and Éric de Lamotte turned a serious risk into an opportunity for staff, giving them control over their future. Their decision proved successful, and IBA's market value increased twelvefold after the company went public. Fortune favors the bold. More importantly, this episode sparked a new dynamic. Although the company was now subject to the responsibilities of a listed firm, its main shareholders remained its driving forces.

The third and final test of resilience, with an even greater impact, was managing rapid growth after the 1998 IPO. In just a few months, the paradigm shifted: from enforced frugality, IBA found itself with a surplus of capital to invest. A series of acquisitions radically transformed the small enterprise, which suddenly became a multinational group. Beyond strategic and managerial considerations, this raised serious questions about the company's culture. How could IBA increase its workforce tenfold without compromising its core values? How could it accommodate new staff and appreciate their contributions? How could it maintain transparency as a publicly traded company facing new confidentiality requirements? How could it move away from a strong Walloon identity and become a multinational organization? How could it foster growth by strengthening managerial skills and organizational maturity?

The managers at the time modestly acknowledged their lack of stature to manage this transition and looked for outside experts. However, none possessed detailed knowledge of an accelerator company's specifics: its cyclical patterns, technical limitations, research expenses, uncertainties, and so on. Although financially practical, their solutions involved compromising too much of IBA's core identity. The efforts failed, raising the question of whether appointing an outsider as CEO could ever be a viable option.

Looking back, this rapid growth was too difficult to handle, especially since it was financed with debt right before a major financial and economic crisis. Also, the decision to expand into service activities around the core business had two effects: it shifted operational control to an American management team and disappointed technology enthusiasts, who saw their expertise pushed aside in favor of operational efficiency and short-term profits. The often-praised functional economy isn't always as relevant as management books suggest. The rest is history: excessive debt forced IBA to sell its sterilization division to focus on the medical sector. However, it didn't have to start over, as the organization had matured and improved performance between 1998 and 2003. From a corporate culture standpoint, though, a "back to basics" approach was necessary.

Strong roots, deep values

During its reorganization in 2004–2005, IBA clarified its position: its purpose was not to maximize short-term shareholder returns. Instead, it embraced a higher mission of protecting, enhancing, and saving lives. It aimed to do so by giving equal importance to the interests of customers, patients, employees, shareholders, and local communities. Planet Earth was later added to form a five-pointed star. While this positioning was not entirely unique, it was forward-thinking. Most companies were only beginning to explore corporate social responsibility (CSR) from a defensive perspective, and very few had committed to a genuine stakeholder approach. IBA thus joined a relatively select group alongside Umicore, Solvay, and Colruyt in Belgium; The Body Shop, Danone, Novo Nordisk, and Unilever in Europe; and Ben & Jerry's, Patagonia, and Interface in the United States.

In a traditional mission statement, four core values were outlined to guide every team member's actions: care, dare, share, and be fair. These simple and memorable values have represented IBA's ethos since it was founded approximately twenty years earlier: caring for patients, customers, and employees, and building trust (care); daring the impossible, facing giants without fear, and investing in the future (dare); combining expertise, sharing knowledge, and working collaboratively (share); and staying fair and transparent, even during tough times (be fair). This powerful statement remains as relevant today as it was two decades ago and continues to motivate the teams.

The sale of the sterilization business and the temporary suspension of the American dream also served as an opportunity to unite around a team that was less culturally diverse but more cohesive. During a memorable meeting, Pierre Mottet voiced his rallying cry: "I'd rather have reliable people than high-flyers. We are the soul of IBA, and we are going to relaunch the project together." The rebuilding process was guided by clear lessons: avoid excessive debt and strategically focus resources on niches where IBA holds an undeniable competitive advantage. As for the opportunity to create a highly diverse management team, that remains uncertain: "It is difficult to attract American or Asian talent to a medium-sized Belgian company. We would like to have more local roots worldwide. On the other hand, there is an advantage to having a small decision-making team that is culturally aligned".[51]

"IBA is a company that isn't comfortable in calm waters."

- Thomas Servais,
President of IBA Industrial Business Unit

COMPASSES FOR THE FUTURE

2

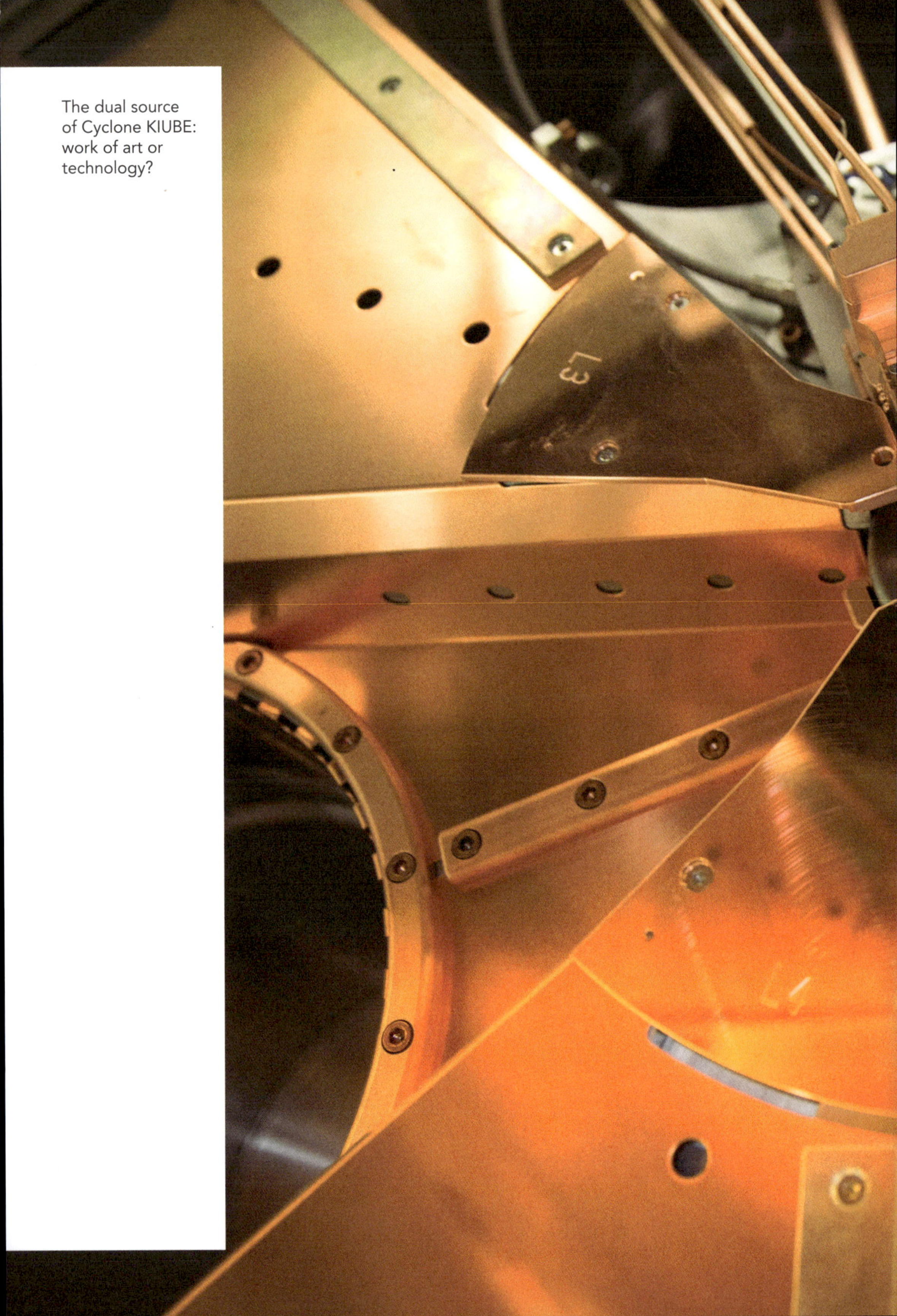

The dual source of Cyclone KIUBE: work of art or technology?

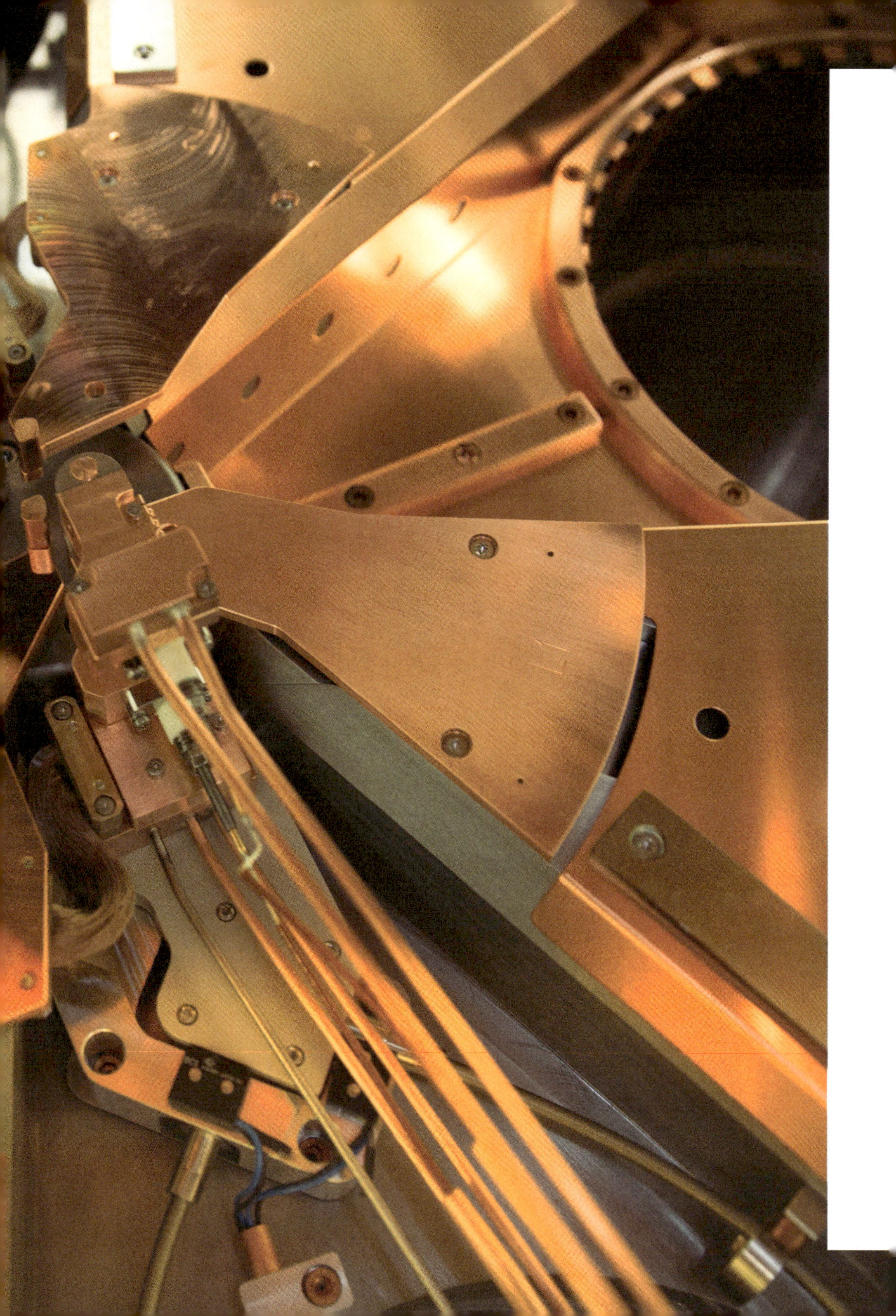

Four permanent features

As we see, IBA has built its management philosophy on core principles, strong convictions, and lessons sometimes learned the hard way. Four guiding compasses have emerged: strategically, only undertake projects where the company possesses a strong competitive advantage, both technically and through its human resources; from a governance perspective, stay at the helm of its own destiny to ensure the corporate purpose stays clear; from an impact perspective, continually improve practices to benefit the common good; and from an operational perspective, be ready to challenge everything whenever circumstances require. These principles inspire current and future employees and managers to stay dedicated to this course, creating sustainable shared value around a meaningful mission.

Irresistible superiority

Frantic innovation

Technological innovation, as poetically described by Philippe de Woot, is the foundation of IBA. Its expertise in accelerators remains unmatched. As one of the few pure players in this field, IBA can offer a complete range of energy and power solutions, which sets it apart in its approach to customers.

While some product lines are industrialized and standardized, such as the Cyclone KIUBE or dosimetry products, others are closer to high-precision craftsmanship, requiring the expertise of entire teams to meet customer specifications—such as the Rhodotron, ProteusPLUS, or ProteusONE. "This is a unique feature that we must accept as such. We approach both products and projects with the same collaborative intelligence, but we recognize that certain aspects of our work still involve a touch of magic".[52] "There is still an artisanal dimension to IBA, in the noble sense of the term. We are like luthiers reproducing the same violin, infusing genius into the repetition of gestures and applying our intellect to what our hands create. This artisanal dimension is close to my heart. I like the idea that we are perceived as the Stradivarius of proton therapy".[53]

Staying ahead of the technological curve is crucial for survival amid intense competition in complex markets. How can we explain IBA's success when competing against prestigious international groups with vastly greater resources in finance, marketing, research, recruitment, and lobbying? For a company mainly active in countries with high labor costs, the essential condition for success lies in "frantic innovation"—a drive to develop the "technology of tomorrow" and to win the battle for competitiveness by focusing on quality. This involves offering high-end products and services that are "a cut above the rest" by combining contractual rigor with close proximity to the client's team.

This approach is especially important as competition comes not only from companies within the same sectors but also from those targeting the same markets with alternative solutions that may be older and less effective but better established. Such is the case with chemotherapy and conventional radiotherapy in oncology, or cobalt and ethylene oxide sterilization.

IBA was not always able to contain its enthusiasm when choosing its battles. Its appetite for risk, entrepreneurial spirit, technological optimism, and desire to build a large industrial group sometimes faced unexpected obstacles or even larger ones than anticipated. The commoditization of FDG, fluctuations in the dollar exchange rate, major financial and political crises, and delays in adopting proton therapy and X-ray sterilization were just some of the many challenges that had to be overcome on the journey toward sustainable profitability. Faced with these uncertainties, IBA gradually developed a clearer sense of strategic positioning, constantly questioning how particle physics engineering could be used to benefit society.

Its drive to innovate and lead in proton therapy has required sacrificing other parts of its business, as it lacked the resources to pursue every venture. This dedication to the medical community and challenging cases—especially children—has been a journey lasting decades, during which IBA has continually innovated in all areas: patient experience, customer service, treatment flow, miniaturization, imaging, dose precision, end-to-end approach, platform architecture, dissemination of clinical knowledge, academic collaborations, financing solutions, and more. With its radically transformative ProteusONE, based on superconductivity, it set a new standard that made proton therapy more accessible. With each step, it gets closer to its goal: giving every cancer patient worldwide the best chance of recovery with the fewest side effects. Young Viggo, affectionately called "the little engine" in-house, embodies this goal. Proton therapy is the most tangible expression of IBA's core purpose—a mission diligently pursued by "artisans of hope".

IBA's original strategy of becoming a diversified technology holding company has been less of a focus in the years following the sale of its sterilization and pharmaceutical divisions and the subsequent shift toward proton therapy starting in 2013. However, with innovations in medical imaging and industrial applications, this balanced approach was reignited in 2023, guided by one key question: "Are we capable of developing an irresistible competitive advantage?" As history has shown, this offers the best opportunity for IBA to achieve healthy and sustained organic growth.

The accelerator-based technology platform offers a wide range of possibilities, making it important to be selective rather than trying to excel in every area at once—especially as regulatory constraints now require more resources than ever. Specifically, IBA aims to serve as an incubator for emerging technologies in niche sectors that have been underexplored due to their highly technical nature. Since the early 2020s, there have been many examples with varying maturity levels: sterilization using the Rhodotron Duo, which can switch between electron beams and X-rays; production of radioisotopes with electron beams; food irradiation; PFAS elimination; partnerships for the targeted production of Actinium-225 and Astatine-211 therapeutic radioisotopes; carbon ion hadron therapy; flash therapy; semiconductor doping, and more. These advanced applications closely align with IBA's mission and have been brought to market with greater selectivity, often through partnerships, by teams with four decades of experience. None of these initiatives guarantees immediate or long-term success, reflecting their highly entrepreneurial nature, but those that succeed will once again enable the people at IBA to say: "We didn't know it was impossible, so we did it."

To reduce uncertainty around long-term technological investments, innovation goes beyond just technical details. IBA has adopted a more integrated commercial strategy across all product lines, providing customers with end-to-end, turnkey solutions. Whether building a radioisotope production facility, a

At its INDux centers, IBA trains its customers and prospects in the use of sterilization equipment, 2024.

proton therapy center, or a sterilization plant, customers benefit from dedicated expertise at every phase. This full support includes permits, profitability analyses, building design, facility certification, digitalization, maintenance, after-sales service, decommissioning, and even renovation. In 2023, IBA signed a contract with Massachusetts General Hospital to manage a full renovation of its very first proton therapy center, launched twenty-two years earlier. By reusing mechanical parts and avoiding the costs of new construction, this project exemplifies the principles of the circular economy. Overall, the value of services keeps growing for IBA, increasing both customer confidence and revenue predictability. Recurring services, which make up one-third of revenues, have strengthened IBA's business model, making it more resilient and stable even during times of lower demand.

Cross-fertilization among business units is another positive effect of the innovative spirit running through the entire organization. Today, dosimetry expertise enhances the efficiency of the proton therapy treatment process; the industrial Rhodotron is now used to produce medical radioisotopes; and a customer in Taiwan, who uses both proton therapy and dosimetry, has discovered the advantages of IBA's sterilization expertise for launching a new business. Although decentralized, IBA maintains a shared technological culture supported by its central research and development team. More experimental projects, undertaken for research laboratories such as MYRRHA and Arronax, and for many years, hadron therapy in Normandy, have only strengthened this expertise. The same applies to the Discovery Lab, inaugurated in 2024, which was designed to rapidly test new ideas from both within and outside the organization.

COUPLER
ELETTA

Collective inventiveness

Innovation only exists because people make it happen. Since its beginning, IBA has always focused on human capital as the key to inventing and reinventing itself. Today, about two-thirds of the staff work in technical, engineering, and R&D roles. The company built itself on a rich pool of talent, centered around a core group of high-level experts whose influence extended well beyond the organization. These prominent figures—some of whom are now members of the fellows' group—shaped a culture of excellence and curiosity that continues to define IBA. To protect this intangible asset, the company put in place mechanisms for knowledge sharing and mentoring, where each mentor trains multiple young "padawans", ensuring the lasting transfer of expertise and team versatility. Over time, experts have become less identifiable as individuals, yet their collective expertise has grown. As Charles Kumps, who led R&D transformation from 2019 to 2024, states: "We had to expand the organization to meet the new challenges of industrialization and reassure the founding experts that we were not planning to phase them out, but that we were working to make them immortal".[54] This approach underscores a strong belief in maintaining a solid internal knowledge base and in "never outsourcing incompetence".

A notable example of this living legacy is the development of the Cyclone KIUBE. As a complete reinvention of the Cyclone 18/9, it was designed by a new generation of engineers without relying on Yves Jongen's expertise. In a symbolic passing of the baton, the young engineers asked him only one favor: his blessing to transform the traditional cylindrical shape of the cyclotron into a cubic form.

Catherine Vandenborre succinctly captures this idea: "A founder is irreplaceable: they embody not only the accumulated knowledge of the company, but also the cultural elements they instill. This is something you cannot replicate; you must continue to promote openness to change and foster a culture of innovation, including working in small teams, without trying to imitate the founder's genius piece by piece. Although Apple never managed to find a replacement for Steve Jobs, it remains hugely successful".[55]

Continuously adapting to changing priorities and scope, the R&D department serves both as a place to develop expertise and as a space for creative stimulation, fueled by an insatiable appetite for new projects—even those that may seem irrational. The Rhodotron TT300-HE was developed out of the firm conviction of the development team, contrary to management's initial stance: "As usual, I made a suggestion, and they did the opposite", jokes Olivier Legrain, always the good sport.

Far from an authoritarian figure, the CEO firmly believes in collective intelligence and every employee's ability to make the right decision when genuine trust is built. Today, IBA does not rely solely on a culture of technical excellence; it remains committed to maintaining the collaborative approach that was key to its initial success. Accessibility, team spirit, and a friendly atmosphere enable employees to "do very serious things very seriously without taking themselves too seriously". The trust placed in each individual, along with high levels of autonomy and free speech, fosters an environment conducive to personal performance. Even tough situations are handled calmly: "What's fantastic about IBA is our ability to get through tough times without stress." This resilience stems from several factors, including Olivier's character, which helps him keep things in perspective kindly and never resort to brusqueness. IBA's leaders share the same curiosity as mad scientists, who see every crisis as a problem to be solved, explains one senior manager. This is how the playful and commitment-driven spirit of a "company that is not comfortable in calm waters" stays alive.

After the COVID-19 pandemic, Olivier Legrain initiated a cultural transformation toward a fully collaborative organization, with transparent, cross-functional goals shared across every department, team, and individual. This approach allowed everyone to continually evaluate their contribution and adjust it as needed. Building on an experiment within the Radiopharma business unit, collective intelligence methods were gradually adopted across the group. The goal was not just to test new ways of working but to embed these structured collaboration practices into a deliberate process that supports IBA's strategic and commercial ambitions. This cultural shift aimed to speed up decision-making and enhance the quality of execution in a context where the organization is diversifying and must respond to a rapidly changing world. It reflects IBA's distinctive entrepreneurial culture of empowerment, initiative, and sharing collective success.

Collective intelligence grows when a group moves beyond just adding opinions and begins to collaborate. It relies on a leader who takes a humble approach, not imposing their vision but instead creating a framework where everyone can contribute. In an environment built on trust, diverse perspectives are valued as sources of wisdom, and transparency is essential for honesty. Decisions are no longer mainly based on hierarchical authority but on consent, enabling progress without hindering collective momentum. Facilitation tools—such as discussion circles, structured brainstorming sessions, open forums, and hackathons—help circulate ideas and debate them until solutions emerge that no one could have found alone.

During the initial learning phase, non-strategic projects focused on principles like integrating new arrivals and organizing team events. After this phase, key topics could be addressed. For example, the organization raised questions such as: "What is the optimal level of profitability that IBA should reach, and how can it be achieved?"; "How can we maximize synergies between the sales and marketing teams in proton therapy?"; "What steps are needed to reorganize the Industrial business unit to meet the five-year goal?"; "How can we better handle complex customer requests by leveraging expertise across the organization?" Support from specially trained internal facilitators helped form groups, which often resulted in practical, targeted solutions.

Therefore, collective intelligence seeks to turn a group's energy into a shared mind capable of innovation and action. When team members expressed skepticism about the approach, Olivier Legrain stated, "I am convinced that collective intelligence has been a real competitive advantage in the past, and that it will be again in the future." The management team summarizes the challenge: "What is admirable about IBA's history is the ingenuity in action mobilized through unique people management. It was collective intelligence before its time: empowering individuals and teams through trust and autonomy. As we continue to grow, decentralizing decisions while remaining accountable is a real business challenge. This has occasionally held us back, especially when navigating cultural differences after merging with other organizations. We must improve in the future by being more inclusive without diluting our way of being".[56]

"IBA remains
an optimistic
innovation driver
and a company that,
because it is innovative,
is both resilient and
takes its share of hits.
I don't imagine
the next 15–20 years
will be a walk
in the park just because
we've suddenly
found wisdom."

- Nicolas Denef,
Head of Proton Therapy Sales Support

Collective intelligence is put into practice through multiple forms of interaction in offices and workshops, 2023.

Olivier Legrain and Pierre Mottet alongside Henri de Romrée, Deputy CEO, 2024.

Charting one's course

The shareholder is always right

While purposeful innovation is IBA's main principle, taking control of its own future is a close second. Pierre and Yves explain: "After the sell-off of many Belgian companies, including those linked to Générale de Belgique, we learned that there was a kind of inevitability for tech start-ups that developed a product before being bought by a large company. This immediately signaled the end of their story. We didn't want to build a start-up just to generate excitement for five or ten years; we wanted to build a long-term business that would create high-quality jobs locally and in many other countries".

As IBA demonstrated, starting a business often involves a hectic launch phase where energy and speed are crucial to prove feasibility and conquer markets. However, while some structures struggle to keep up with this pace, a long-lasting company goes through several consolidation phases: financial security, governance reinforcement, growth stabilization, and knowledge transfer. This shift from a sprint to a marathon requires maintaining strong control of shareholdings. As long as the founders or long-term shareholders remain in charge, the company can stay true to its mission, invest in its talent, and prioritize continuous innovation over passing trends. This ability to control their own destiny, combined with the capacity to adapt, enables them to turn initial success into a lasting collective journey.

The 1996 purchase of 62 percent of the shares by a majority of employees and directors, amid the threat of a hostile takeover, proved crucial in IBA's history. The takeover bid revealed that the supposed loyalty of long-standing partners was not unanimous. If IBA aimed to pursue a project beyond its immediate financial interests, it had to stay in control of its own future. As Pierre wisely notes: "Since the shareholder is always right, we had to become the majority shareholder." Instead of a traditional management buyout, the leadership triumvirate—Pierre, Éric, and Yves—chose a solution that upheld the founding spirit of IBA. The project couldn't be theirs alone; it had to involve the entire staff. By opening the buyout to the staff, they turned a traditional scheme into a collective act of faith in the future. Over 60 percent of the team responded positively, making Belgian Anchorage a project with majority support.

Although the prospects for returns seemed very uncertain, with no IPO scheduled at the time, the operation was planned for the long run. To maintain lasting control, the exit conditions for Belgian Anchorage were intentionally strict. The arrangement resisted temptations—including the allure of selling when the stock price hit its peak—and enabled the company to respond strongly, sometimes through debt, to endure challenges. Since then, Pierre, in particular, has worked hard to ensure that IBA's articles of association offer a strong defense against any future attempts.

During the excitement of the late 1990s, listing on the stock exchange attracted capital and boosted global visibility. However, IBA's stock market performance often resembled a roller coaster, reflecting the economy's fluctuations, the cyclical patterns of its markets, and the occasionally disappointing expectations surrounding its bold entrepreneurial ventures. To address this, management decided to focus on long-term stability: strengthening recurring revenues, stabilizing its services, and building on its competitive strengths, all while investing in growth and innovation.

This strategy did not come without challenges. The 1996 leveraged employee buyout was powered by high debt and substantial risk taken by investors. The entry of Tenet and the IPO helped reduce the company's debt. Belgian Anchorage's stake in IBA dropped to 42 percent and then quickly to 27 percent after consecutive capital increases in 1999 and 2000. The following year, Tenet Healthcare's hasty exit caused Belgian Anchorage to incur significant debt again to buy back these shares. Dilutions were addressed through effective statutory protections designed to guard the company from hostile takeover attempts: by the end of the financial crisis between 2001 and 2003, when IBA was forced to sell its sterilization business, the company's net cash position was three times higher than its market capitalization, which could have made it an easy target for competitors.

Dividends received from IBA and the sale of certain shares subsequently enabled the repayment of the debt incurred during the Tenet divestment, placing Belgian Anchorage in a strong, stable position for the future. The dividend policy was designed to reward loyal, long-term shareholders.

In 2020, after adding the stakeholder approach to IBA's articles of incorporation, long-term shareholders received double voting rights. Renamed Sustainable Anchorage, the holding company increased its influence in decision-making with 30 percent of the voting rights. The consistent influx of new institutional investors afterward stabilized the shareholder base and decreased the free float to less than 40 percent.

While "the shareholder is always right", their power is subject to good governance rules. Since Belgian Anchorage took control, IBA immediately adopted an open, structured, and demanding governance framework. The involvement of major private equity players brought a high level of professionalism and discipline to management. When IBA decided to open its capital to the public in 1998, it complemented this structure with legal guarantees of transparency, control, and compliance, as mandated by law and the corporate governance code for listed companies. Within this framework, the Board of Directors distinguished itself by its strict approach: although law requires that one-third of directors be independent, IBA often had more than half. Recruited globally for their expertise, these directors are tasked with reviewing, challenging, and supporting management, while ensuring the interests of all stakeholders are protected. This duty is clearly outlined in the charter signed by each director upon their appointment: a pledge to monitor, advise, and energize the company in line with its mission, stakeholder model, and values.

Transmitting heritage

Sustainable Anchorage was created to transfer the company's responsibility to future IBA colleagues, rather than to heirs disconnected from the entrepreneurial effort. Pierre states: "We are still only the first generation. The second generation is glad to be here but hasn't had to make the same sacrifices we did. We don't want our children to inherit this company; we want decision-making authority to stay with those currently involved, who will be the entrepreneurs of tomorrow. These eternally youthful teams, eager to start new projects, won't have to worry about their shareholders selling the company, as we nearly did."

This transmission took place on a small scale during the first twenty years. In 2020, the creation of Management Anchorage—an investment platform for executives—and its acquisition of a 21 percent stake in Sustainable Anchorage in 2024, replacing some longstanding stakeholders, sped up the process, and broadened capital access to about fifty IBA managers and employees. This allowed them to gain direct representation within the reference shareholder and, indirectly, within IBA. It represents a move toward a certain form of self-determination, aligned with the values of daring, caring, sharing, and fairness. Through this mechanism, IBA's role as an incubator for niche innovations, focused on a targeted group of growth accelerators, can be cemented over the long term.

In the long run, the question remains whether this protection can be extended to all employees worldwide. The steward ownership model, used by companies like Bosch, Novo Nordisk, Zeiss, and Patagonia, provides inspiration. By separating corporate governance from purely financial interests, it allows companies to focus on long-term value creation rather than short-term gains. Under this model, voting rights are granted to a foundation or a group of "guardians", usually made up of executives, employees, or independent figures, who are responsible for protecting the company's vision and values. Profits continue to fairly reward investors or heirs, with a portion systematically reinvested to strengthen the business, support innovation, or generate positive impact. Although it hasn't formally adopted this model, IBA follows a similar principle. It is listed on the stock exchange but has strong backing from Sustainable Anchorage, giving it an uncommon hybrid governance structure: a company open to financial markets, yet with its core protected by committed shareholders to ensure that economic performance never undermines its societal impact.

The question of succession also arises internally, among teams, especially within the management team. In 2012, after several unsuccessful attempts to hand over the reins to external CEOs, the transition from the long-standing management duo to Olivier Legrain involved a thoughtful process of role allocation, with Yves and Pierre remaining on board as part of an executive triumvirate dedicated to the company's values and mission. In 2023, Henri de Romrée joined the three to form a quartet. While the operational division of roles remains clear between Olivier and Henri, Henri's appointment as Deputy CEO has prepared him to take the lead after gaining sufficient time to develop a deep understanding of the company and to carry its spirit forward. "I joined IBA because of its positive impact on the world, with people at its core, it has a commitment to values, purpose, and sustainability, and this is unequivocal", says Henri.

Serving the common good

Beyond profit

The world has changed significantly since IBA was founded in 1986. The planet now supports three billion more people, who live about ten years longer on average. The Human Development Index has risen from 0.57 to 0.73, fueled by progress in major developing countries, especially in Asia. Global wealth (GDP) has increased by 7.5 times in real terms.

Yet, despite these notable advances, inequalities persist: global imbalances have barely diminished, and changing lifestyles now lead to 19 million new cancer cases each year—twice as many as in 1986. Despite major medical breakthroughs, the disease remains the second leading cause of death worldwide.

More broadly, the interconnectedness between humans and the rest of the living world—what philosopher Bruno Latour calls "the Terrestrial"—has felt the full force of the "great acceleration". In just four decades, atmospheric CO_2 levels have climbed from 348 to over 420 parts per million, increasing global temperatures by 1.4°C compared to the pre-industrial era. Of the nine planetary boundaries identified by the Stockholm Resilience Centre, seven have now been exceeded, endangering ecosystem resilience and Earth's habitability for many species, including humans.[57]

In the face of such upheaval, humanity responds in various ways: denial, apathy, withdrawal—or proactive action. The last option is the most demanding, often hindered by what could be called the "triangle of inaction": governments, citizens, and businesses shirk responsibility, hiding behind endless debates —international competition, "end of the world versus end of the month", greenwashing, technosolutionism, or post-growth—further delaying the essential and critical shift.

In a time when "the old world is dying, and the new world is slow to emerge", pioneers light the way. IBA's history demonstrates that a company can drive societal progress. For nearly forty years, its mission to apply both pure and applied science to healthcare has inspired its teams to go above and beyond.

Since 2004, IBA has aimed higher than just the direct contribution of its products and services by adopting a stakeholder approach. Customers, patients, suppliers, employees, shareholders, local communities—and, since 2015, the environment—form an interconnected ecosystem. In this model, no party should dominate at the expense of others: while recognizing the importance of sound profitability, balance and consistency guide action, rather than a simple pursuit of immediate profit. The green cells' experiences demonstrate that tangible improvements are possible anywhere and that they can come together to bring about meaningful change. However, the process following the activation of these green cells has not been straightforward, involving learning, assessment, and reimagining. As Pierre Mottet explains: "We made gradual progress because our managerial resources did not allow us to cover all areas. But these issues have become increasingly important on the agenda. Today, we have invested and are recognized as one of the best large B Corp companies."

In his opening message of the 2020 annual report, Olivier Legrain affirmed: "The role of the company goes far beyond maximizing its profits." He reiterated the importance of balancing stakeholders' interests. Saving lives through proton therapy, investing in the well-being of employees, or maintaining customer relationships on the other side of the world—each of these actions incurs a cost and causes various impacts. IBA's task is to strike the right balance, ensuring that no aspect is sacrificed for the benefit of another alone. In this context, profit still plays a vital role, much like blood in the body, in funding long-term growth, rewarding shareholders, and supporting the company's purpose.

Teams gathered to focus on the theme of sustainability, 2017.

Meeting with the winners of the Hera Awards, recognizing academic work proposing sustainable solutions, awarded by the Foundation for Future Generations with the support of IBA, 2023.

In this spirit, IBA consistently aims to serve the common good by improving the health of millions of patients, lowering its environmental impact, and creating shared value with its stakeholders. A stable, non-speculative shareholder base supports this long-term strategy, regardless of market trends, reversals, or short-term financial pressures. This enables the company to stand firm in its convictions—even when facing more cynical investors—that a business set to succeed in the future will inevitably be sustainable.

Far from being naive or idealistic, this commitment supports both ethical and strategic goals. Focusing on sustainability helps reduce risks, attract and keep talented people seeking purpose, optimize resource use, anticipate future regulatory limits, and enter new markets. "There isn't even any internal tension on the subject; it's become a given", says Olivier Legrain.

IBA aims to show in practice that the public good and the company's interests can naturally align. Sustainability goes beyond superficial statements; it is built into the very mechanisms of the organization, extending beyond the minimum requirements of legal compliance. Self-restraint has become a core principle, reflected in the company's articles of association, embedded in the role of the board of directors, integrated into processes, and woven into everyday culture. As Olivier Legrain notes, "Creativity and imagination are more fertile under constraint. Self-restraint is, in fact, a way of giving oneself an advantage".[58]

One clear example today is IBA's approach to decarbonization. Recognizing that completely eliminating operational greenhouse gas emissions is currently not feasible, the company works to address the remaining emissions to achieve climate neutrality. Among various methods—whose scientific rigor varies—IBA has chosen to support European initiatives that promote the transition to regenerative agricultural practices. This effort aims not only to reduce emissions

within agricultural systems but also to strengthen the climate resilience of local food supply chains. Through its partnership with Soil Capital, another B Corp, IBA helps farmers incorporate legumes into their crop rotations. These crops, which can fix atmospheric carbon dioxide, play a crucial role in lowering emissions, improving soil fertility, and maintaining yields. "Our goal is not to buy cheap certificates to soothe our guilty conscience, but to participate in an innovative revolution in this field", explains Olivier Legrain.

First obtained in 2021, B Corp certification recognizes these efforts and encourages new initiatives. In 2024, the second certification showed a significant improvement in operational impact. This benchmark helps measure, compare, improve, and promote positive change. It is not just a product or service that receives this certification, but the entire company in all its aspects. Joining this movement of "companies for the common good" also means becoming part of an international community of nearly 10,000 companies operating in more than 100 countries, all advocating for a different way of doing business.

This commitment goes beyond the company and is shown in the career paths of its leaders. Pierre Mottet has used his expertise and social vision to promote a prosperous and sustainable Wallonia through his roles as president of Invest.BW, Agoria Wallonia, and the MecaTech cluster at its start. He also helped develop impact startups through the SEn'SE fund, and in 2021, he became president of the Union Wallonne des Entreprises (UWE), now called AKT for Wallonia. From 2007 to 2019, Yves Jongen was president of the MecaTech fund, which fosters innovation in mechanical engineering. Olivier Legrain is involved in several startups, networks, and NGOs that support sustainability. Alongside Pierre Mottet, Sybille van den Hove, and Jacques Crahay, he co-founded the CEO association "2030", a forum for business leaders committed to fighting climate change and pushing for sustainable transition. As administrator Marcel Miller notes, "These are people whose convictions go far beyond their companies, and who put incredible energy into rallying those around them to make things happen for their region".[59]

Towards holistic impact

Today, powerful tools and frameworks allow us to evaluate the positive and negative effects of organizations. These approaches prompt us to look beyond financial metrics and adopt a systemic view—one that considers environmental, social, and societal impacts. Core principles include identifying what truly matters to the company and its stakeholders, combining quantitative data with qualitative insights, and ensuring transparency through independent verification. Although these methods still face challenges—like the complexity of value chains and the proliferation of standards—they share a common belief: progress starts with measurement, and the future of sustainable business relies on the ability to report honestly and transparently on all impacts.

At IBA, impact extends beyond just financial performance or technological efficiency. The company sees impact as a dynamic system where people, the planet, and society interact and influence each other. Today, IBA aims to incorporate this systemic approach into every innovation, every organizational decision, and daily activity. Although there are still imperfections, the coherence of this vision requires that financial returns align with broader values: the variable part of management pay linked to sustainability progress now matches the other two aspects—order intake, which secures future viability, and annual profitability.

IBA's environmental awareness is based on the belief that the right to a healthy environment is inseparable from the fundamental right to life. That is why the planet has become one of the company's five key stakeholders. The entire value chain is being gradually considered, from raw material extraction to recycling end-of-life equipment—even as visibility decreases further from the core business. Upstream, IBA prioritizes responsible sourcing and efficient resource use, fully aware that steel, alloys, composites, and electronic components have a significant environmental impact. Within its operations, the company emphasizes safety and efficiency, from assembly to testing and logistics. Responsibility doesn't end at delivery: IBA supports customers through maintenance and updates, sometimes extending equipment lifespan beyond thirty years. Finally, the company explores reuse or dismantling options and actively encourages material recycling.

Through its partnership with Soil Capital, IBA assists local farmers as they move towards regenerative agricultural practices.

The Rhodotron TT300HE was designed using eco-friendly design principles; its power consumption is reduced thanks to pulsed technology.

IBA addresses the complex issue of climate change by covering everything from direct emissions at manufacturing sites to the carbon footprint of equipment used by customers. Emissions from scopes 1 and 2—such as heating, electricity, and company vehicles—are reduced through a 100 percent electric mobility policy, incentives for alternative transportation like bike leasing, on-site solar power, and renewable electricity. However, most of IBA's carbon footprint is in Scope 3: the use of its products, which mainly depends on the electricity mix of the countries where its customers operate.

Aware of the physical and transition risks associated with climate change, IBA has incorporated them into its strategic analysis and is turning these challenges into opportunities for differentiation. Eco-design has become a central part of innovation. The company aims to integrate environmental considerations into product design, reducing their footprint at every stage of the life cycle. This approach merges clinical performance with sustainability, ensuring solutions that deliver equal or better service while minimizing environmental impact. To accomplish this, IBA encourages team awareness, the adoption of specific design rules, and the use of internal data to evaluate the actual footprint of its equipment. Eight principles support this approach, including reducing energy use, increasing system lifespan, decreasing waste, and promoting recycling. This philosophy results in tangible innovations across the portfolio: thanks to superconductivity, the ProteusONE proton therapy system consumes much less energy than its predecessor; the Cyclone KIUBE and IntegraLab One combine compactness with energy efficiency; the Rhodotron provides an electric alternative to traditional sterilization methods, eliminating associated toxic waste. Its pulsed technology also decreases consumption. Beyond its products, IBA considers all its operations: digitalization, mobility, reverse logistics. Finally, in partnership with EcoVadis, the company involves its suppliers in this effort by assessing their practices and setting continuous improvement goals.

From a social impact perspective, IBA is dedicated to creating a safe and motivating work environment where safety, well-being, and work-life balance are prioritized. Through its 'At Our Best' human resources framework, IBA uses practical tools to foster dialogue, enhance skills, and share the value created.

The approach is based on a "promise" to employees: the chance to innovate, find purpose and impact in their work, grow personally and professionally, work independently, and help create a warm, collaborative environment. In return for employees' dedication, IBA offers trust, recognition, and a culture that supports both individual and collective success. In 2020, a financial recognition scheme with significant symbolic value was launched: a profit-sharing plan for all staff, where every euro paid to shareholders is matched by a euro paid to employees. The high number of applicants for open positions and the low staff turnover —about 5 percent—show the success of this approach.

Diversity, equity, and inclusion are actively promoted every day. Differences are seen not as barriers but as drivers of creativity and innovation. Common challenges in this area are acknowledged and addressed, including the dominance of the Belgian informal network and headquarters, the underrepresentation of women and non-Belgians in senior management, unconscious biases, and difficulties in attracting a diverse talent pool. Promoting a collaborative and inclusive culture further strengthens this effort.

An ecosystem based on trust

IBA's holistic approach to business emphasizes promoting the common good that goes beyond its own boundaries. The company succeeds when its entire ecosystem thrives—a mutually beneficial arrangement that includes patient experience, regional development, supplier relationships, academic partnerships, and, most importantly, customer success.

IBA's mission is truly meaningful only if it benefits patients. The numbers are impressive: from 2001 to 2025, over 150,000 patients have been treated with its proton therapy equipment. More than 700 of its accelerators installed worldwide produce the radioisotopes necessary for diagnosing millions and provide sterilization solutions that save lives. Over 10,000 healthcare professionals depend on IBA's dosimetry solutions to ensure the quality of imaging and treatment doses administered to patients. When projects are carried out in emerging markets like Myanmar, Egypt, or sub-Saharan African countries, profit margins are adjusted to match local conditions. Simpler, less expensive technical solutions—such as the Cyclone KEY released in 2022—also improve accessibility. Its compact size allows hospitals to produce fewer key isotopes locally, including N-13 ammonia for detecting cardiovascular disease. This enables IBA to expand its range of cyclotrons to lower energies while making PET technology accessible to countries that previously could not access it, especially in Africa.

Behind every innovation, every proton therapy room installed, every radioisotope produced, and every product sterilized, there are human faces and personal journeys. Even if patients are sometimes the distant "customer of the customer", they remain central to IBA's mission. The design and environment of the treatment rooms were created in collaboration with Philips to help reduce patient stress. Today, the Clinical Affairs department continues its efforts to

Pictures by Yves
Founder
SPANESI
iba

The Oncia Community Foundation and Fundació Kalida are joining forces to develop integrative cancer care centers at major Spanish hospitals, 2024.

Engineering students visiting the Beam Factory, 2023.

User meetings provide great opportunities for sharing and networking. Here, the event in Philadelphia, USA, in 2015.

make proton therapy more accessible by sharing scientific evidence that shows this technique results in better outcomes and fewer side effects than traditional methods across more indications. Additionally, a patient's journey goes far beyond the technical aspects of treatment. Based on this belief, the Oncia Community Foundation aims to provide holistic support to patients battling cancer.[60] Another foundation, Oncidium—strongly supported by IBA—raises awareness about theranostics and encourages its broader adoption.

IBA has consistently aimed to be a socially responsible company by actively supporting the development of the territories where it operates. Its close relationship with Walloon Region authorities dates back to its early days, with these authorities playing a key role in establishing IBA and later offering targeted subsidies and recoverable advances to support its research. In return, IBA has provided attractive career opportunities to many engineers, technicians, and employees from nearby educational institutions. This dynamic has since expanded globally. "I am just as proud to create quality jobs in India as I am in Wallonia", says Olivier Legrain. For every internal position, IBA generates three to four times as many jobs among its suppliers, most of whom have formed long-term partnerships with the company, making organizational boundaries increasingly permeable: Jema for power electronics, Karl Hugo for precision mechanics, Aeriane for composite components, Ateliers de la Meuse for rotating gantries delivered directly to clients, and more. As a virtual factory assembling subsystems from partner suppliers, IBA emphasizes the importance of these relationships.

IBA has also built a network of mutually beneficial partnerships with academic institutions. The first was, naturally, the Catholic University of Louvain. When IBA was launched, several faculties were approached: physics, chemistry, medicine, civil engineering, management, and the central administration. Since then, IBA has been cited as an example in many courses, and, to this day, continues to provide opportunities for young graduates who only need to "cross the street" to start their careers. UCL still owns a small stake in IBA's capital.[61]

IBA's partnerships with the academic world extend far beyond Louvain-la-Neuve. In Belgium, most universities today have begun discussions with IBA to advance proton therapy, while the IRE and SCK-CEN—two public utility foundations—have long partnered with IBA in nuclear medicine. Across Europe, IBA often acts as a technology provider, collaborating with prestigious laboratories on major research initiatives, including the Maestro program on cancer treatment equipment (2004–2009), the Raddel program on nanosurgery (2011–2013), the Life program on SF_6 substitution, and others. Globally, IBA has established specific partnerships with leading research institutions. PBS was developed in collaboration with Massachusetts General Hospital and the University of Pennsylvania. Since 2019, the Flash method has been explored through several projects with UPenn, the Institut Curie in Paris, University Medical Center of Groningen in the Netherlands, the University of Washington, and the Fred Hutchinson Cancer Center in Seattle. Launched in 2022, the Protect-Trial clinical research study on esophageal cancer united nineteen industrial and academic partners across eight countries. Lastly, IBA has created globally renowned academies that bring together the world's most advanced universities and clinical centers in its fields of expertise, organizing formal meetings and structured training courses. These public-private partnerships hold commercial importance while advancing science and technology.

Last but not least, the customer is a vital part of the trust chain that defines the IBA ecosystem. Over time, the company has built very close relationships with certain key clients. More broadly, IBA supplies highly advanced, strategically crucial equipment to its customers—technology that helps them achieve high, stable productivity across sectors. The durability of these machines requires forming truly long-term partnerships. IBA and its customers do much more than just complete a commercial transaction; they have a decades-long relationship. Their teams develop exceptionally close working bonds. As Marcel Miller summarizes: "After-sales service is absolutely essential in these activities. If a machine breaks down, it costs daily and impacts patient care. You have to be extremely responsive. You must excel during initial installation, at startup, and throughout the entire lifecycle. This is something IBA does exceptionally well".[62] Jean-Louis Bol agrees: "We are in the same boat with our customers. We take every possible step to reduce risk in their projects. From the start, we pay close attention to contract language. We always aim to include all necessary conditions for a successful relationship in the contract. We even insist that customers read it carefully, so they understand all the ins and outs".[63] This very special relationship is especially tangible during user meetings—annual events organized since 1996 by each business unit at a client site—where experience sharing is extremely productive, and the atmosphere is friendly.

The only constant is change

Maintaining a sustainable competitive advantage, controlling one's destiny, and working for the common good are three intangible elements carefully cultivated in IBA's long-term journey. Yet a fourth reality asserts itself in every enterprise—especially those operating within the global high-tech medical market: the need to adapt to change and the capacity to rethink everything when reality disrupts even the most well-laid plans.

A Volatile, Uncertain, Complex, and Ambiguous world

IBA operates in an exciting environment, yet one filled with uncertainty and real risks. The main strategic challenge is whether to invest in innovative technologies, knowing that a prototype might prove unstable or be overtaken by competing innovations, or to support promising developments that may not be profitable. Stability also depends on the women and men behind these projects; losing key experts could temporarily weaken the business. Even if IBA faces no direct competitors across its markets, it competes with giants with substantial resources, and a technological breakthrough could make some of its solutions obsolete. Additionally, because equipment is tied to healthcare reimbursement, each country's policies directly influence the order book.

From an operational perspective, a single proton therapy order can shift the entire year's balance; stocks of technological components are susceptible to becoming obsolete; and new products, tested directly on site, must be quickly adjusted for non-compliance. Additionally, quality and safety constraints can impede system acceptance or even lead to legal action. Regulatory obligations demand significant compliance efforts, especially since each market has its own lengthy and revocable approval processes. From a legal standpoint, the company must defend itself against risks of corruption, intellectual property infringement, and litigation, particularly in markets like the United States, where litigation culture is strong. In proton therapy, unsuccessful bidders often challenge public procurement procedures. Over the years, several disputes have burdened IBA's management, including the breakdown of the partnership with CPS for PET cyclotrons, the customer's refusal to accept the Essen proton therapy project, and attempts by Optivus and Titan to dispute ownership of IBA's technologies.

The economic climate introduces additional unpredictability. Interest rates, currency fluctuations, and commodity inflation directly impact manufacturing costs and project profitability. Several times, IBA was affected by the devaluation of the dollar or the yen against the euro. Reliance on complex global supply chains can cause significant project delays, as seen during the COVID-19 pandemic. Sometimes, the global financial system wavers, slowing investments in healthcare and freezing bank credit lines. This was exactly the case for IBA when the internet and technology bubble burst between 2001 and 2003, forcing the company to halt its sterilization projects. Similarly, around 2010, limited financing following the subprime crisis led the company to abandon its radiopharmaceutical development. Although the strategic goals remained sound and were successfully pursued by other owners, they no longer aligned with IBA's available resources.

To mitigate these risks, IBA gradually implemented comprehensive measures: strict R&D and hypercare processes for its customers to ensure the reliability of its innovations, diligent inventory monitoring, flexible sourcing, diversification of activities and markets, ethical governance through a reinforced code of conduct, appropriate contractual arrangements, and insurance coverage, international quality certifications, and ongoing regulatory oversight. This combination of controlled innovation, prevention, insurance, and transparency aims to safeguard the company's financial stability and reputation, while maintaining the trust of its customers, partners, and authorities.

These risks are more than just theoretical; they push the company to innovate constantly, promote knowledge sharing, and stay alert in a competitive global landscape. These factors make its path both challenging and unique. They create a culture where uncertainty is not seen as a crippling threat, but as a starting point.

Staying on track or straying off-path?

Confronting these uncertainties, many of which can stack up and create a cumulative impact, the best approach is to rely on core principles while staying open to re-evaluating everything as reality catches up with dreams. Staying alert, avoiding complacency, and maintaining a willingness to take risks are key traits of IBA's leaders, managers, and team members.

Several times, the company was forced to reorganize, which sometimes caused fatigue among employees facing constant change. These back-and-forth shifts, seen as sudden and unexpected, occasionally wore down employees who lacked a full understanding of the situation, as was the case with the successive transformation plans carried out between 2016 and 2023, modeled after market fluctuations with a delayed effect. In such circumstances, values, transparency, and collective intelligence remain assets for navigating chaotic periods.

Strategically, the path paved over forty years will not lead to a status quo tomorrow. The scars that have hardened the skin of the first generation should motivate the next, not hinder it. "At the executive level, there is a very strong survival spirit. Having been through so many crises, they understand the value of what has been built", says Thomas Servais. "I came to terms with the fact that a company was not immortal so that I wouldn't despair if that were to happen", admits Yves Jongen. As for Pierre Mottet, some claim that he adopted the motto 'Only the paranoid survive,' in reference to the many burning issues he was forced to resolve.

Although history inspires, it should not constrain. What role does risk play? What boundaries are acceptable for prudence in this highly-regulated environment? "People must be encouraged to take risks, even if it involves making mistakes. We still have a long way to go in understanding failure. When something doesn't succeed, we are not brave enough to conduct post-mortem analysis", notes Yves Jongen. "This is how to become a learning organization, through systematic feedback", adds Olivier Legrain.

History plays a vital role at IBA, just like in any other organization. Early strategic choices—such as selecting proton therapy or setting up a base in Louvain-la-Neuve—shaped the company's identity and future direction. This aligns with the principle of path dependency: once a certain skill, structure, or infrastructure is established, it becomes difficult to change because the entire ecosystem—experts, customers, and partners—has developed around it. That's why some strategic paths continue for long periods, even when new options become available.

Nevertheless, loyalty to the path is not unavoidable. While IBA's history offers valuable experience, it should not become a trap. The challenge is to stay true to its core identity while also exploring new directions and questioning current practices. To avoid being hindered by the past, it is important to maintain the agility of a pioneer, even after many chapters have been written. In 2016, the question arose of whether to sell the dosimetry business, despite its successful integration. In 2024, IBA announced plans to relaunch radioisotope production with PanTera, even though this type of downstream activity had not been pursued since 2013. Who knows—perhaps tomorrow the principles of limiting debt or pursuing external growth could be questioned.

In today's unpredictable world, the success of sustainable governance relies on the ability to expand one's perspective and reconcile seemingly conflicting realities: short-term and long-term; profit and purpose; performance and robustness. Day after day, IBA demonstrates its unwavering commitment to this path.

The NGC1097 galaxy, photographed by Yves Jongen, ... or how to reconcile the infinitesimally small and the infinitely large.

APPENDICES

Activities of IBA since its inception

1. Medical imaging

Subfields	Activities/products
Nuclear medicine/SPECT	Cyclone 30, Cyclone 70, IKON, targets, and associated chemistry systems
TEP (Positron Emission Tomography)	Cyclone 10/5, Cyclone 18/9, Cyclone 3D, KIUBE, KEY
Dosimetry for imaging	Quality assurance solutions for medical scanners
Radioisotope production	FDG, other PET radiotracers, and radiopharmaceutical support
Other related systems	Radiopharmaceutical quality control, phantoms, calibration tools

2. Radiotherapy

Subfields	Activities/products
Proton therapy	Proteus 235, ProteusPLUS, ProteusONE; Pencil Beam Scanning (PBS); IMPT; Adaptive PT; DynamicARC, ConformalFLASH
Radiotherapy	Microtron Racetrack MM50
Neutron therapy	Occasional historical participation (Belgium, Japan)
Brachytherapy	Production of radioisotopes for Theragenics and IBt, Radiocoil, Visicoil
Technique & QA	Dosimetry systems for radiotherapy (IBA Dosimetry)
Software solutions	Collaboration with TPS (treatment planning systems) suppliers

3. Theranostics

Subfields	Activities/products
High-energy cyclotrons	Cyclone 30XP and Cyclone 70, particularly for the production of astatine-211
Integrated production of therapeutic radioisotopes	Emerging therapeutic radioisotopes, PanTera (lutetium-177, actinium-225)
Related technologies	Advanced high-power targets, production optimization

4. Industrial applications

Subfields	Activities/products
Sterilization	Rhodotron; sterilization of medical devices; food pasteurization; anthrax treatment
Material modification	Cable treatment (Rhodotron, Dynamitron RDI); semiconductor doping; engine wear measurement (IDS spin-off); microfiltration membranes (IP4IT spin-off); oil refining (unsuccessful)
Inspection & security	Eurotunnel and port cargo scanning projects (unsuccessful)
Dose applications	Beam measurement systems and industrial quality assurance

5. Research equipment and technologies

Subfields	Activities/products
Ion sources	ECR sources, specialized sources for fundamental research in nuclear physics
Electromagnetic separators	Xenon isotope separator (for the IRE)
Other developments	Research cyclotrons; radiofrequency amplifiers for laboratories; magnets; radiofrequency cavities; injectors; specialized subsystems

IBA in figures

Revenue [1986-2024]

millions €

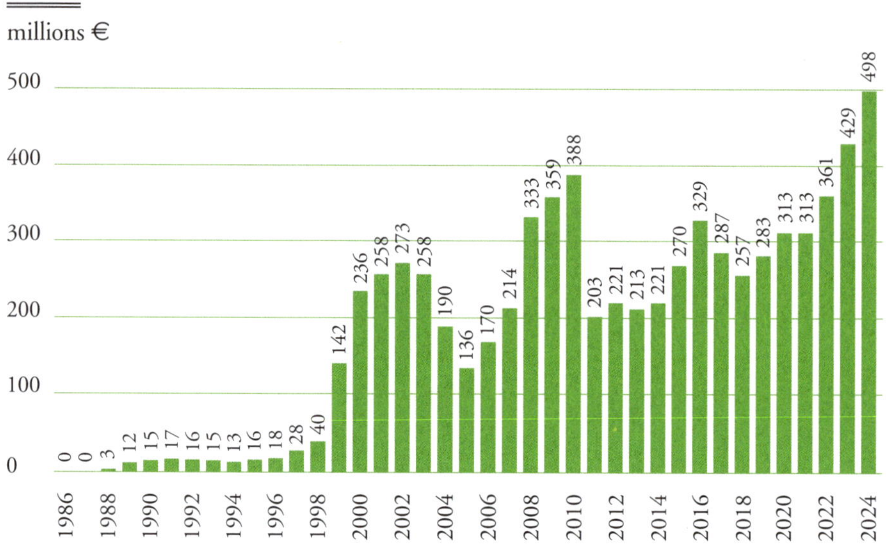

Net result [1986-2024]

millions €

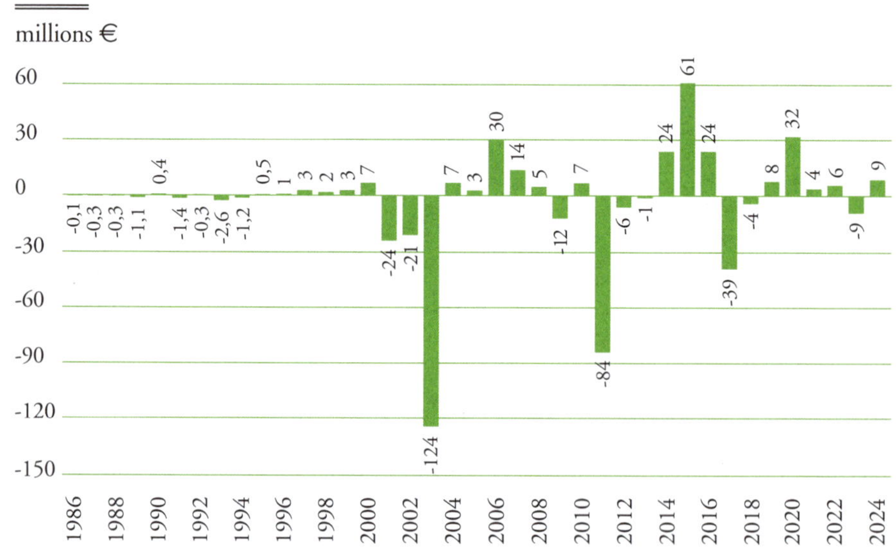

Market capitalization [1997-2024]

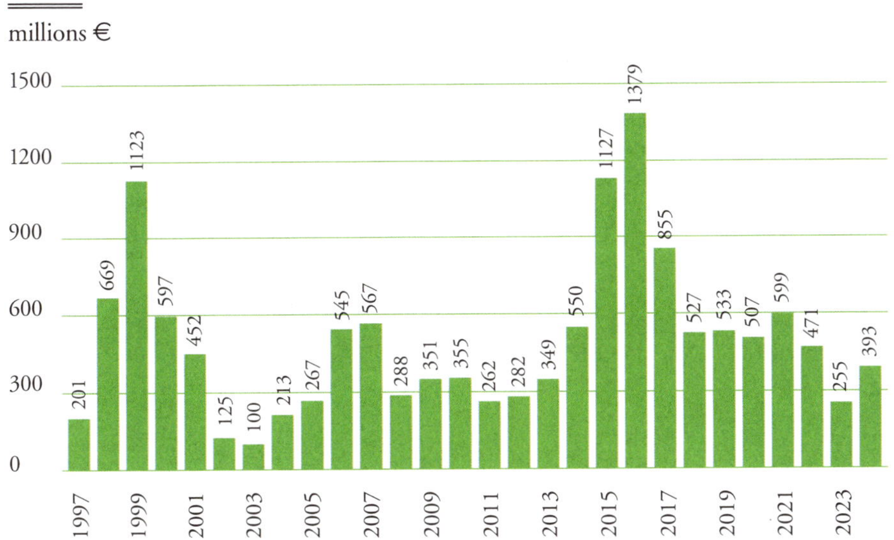

Headcount [1986-2024]

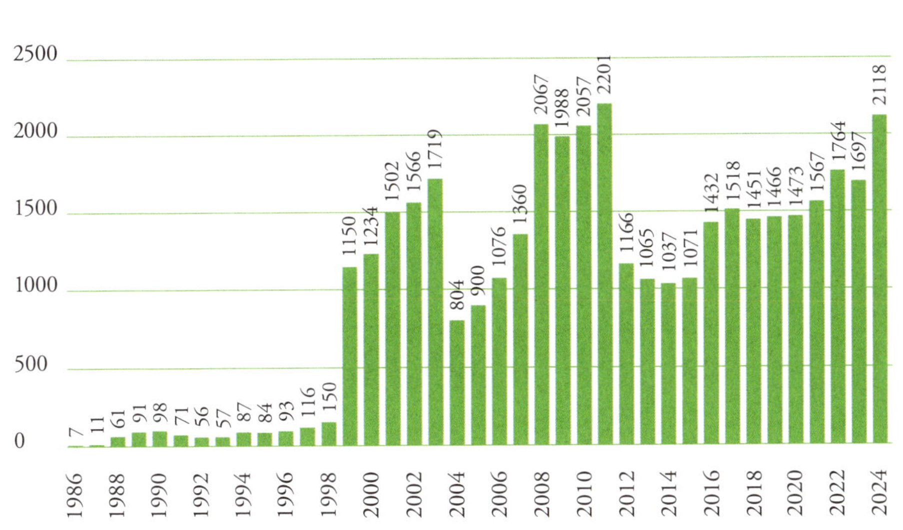

List of acronyms

ACEC – Ateliers de Constructions Électriques de Charleroi
ASTRO – American Society for Radiation Oncology
BBL – Banque Bruxelles Lambert
B Corp – Benefit Corporation
BU – Business Unit
CBCT – Cone Beam Computed Tomography (tomodensitométrie à faisceau conique)
CEA – Commissariat à l'Énergie Atomique French Atomic Energy Commission
CEAEN – Centre d'Études pour les Applications de l'Énergie Nucléaire Centre for the Study of Nuclear Energy Applications
CEO – Chief Executive Officer
CFO – Chief Financial Officer
CGN – China General Nuclear Power Group
CGNNT – CGN Nuclear Technology Application
CGR-MeV – Compagnie Générale de Radiologie – Mégaélectronvolt
CO_2 – Carbon dioxide
COO – Chief Operating Officer
CPS – CTI Pet Systems Inc. (Subsidiary of CTI)
CRC – Centre de Recherches du Cyclotron (UCL) Cyclotron Research Centre
CRO – Chief Research Officer
CTI – Computer Technology and Imaging Inc
CYCLONE – CYClotron de LOuvain-la-NEuve
EASDAQ - European Association of Securities Dealers Automatic Quotation System
EBCO – Eppich & Burger Manufacturing Company
ECR – Electron-Cyclotron Resonance ion source
ESTRO – European Society for Radiotherapy and Oncology
FAFER – Fabrique de Fer de Charleroi
FDA – Food and Drug Administration
FDG – Fluorodeoxyglucose
GANIL – Grand Accélérateur National d'Ions Lourds Large Heavy Ion National Accelerator
GMS – Griffith Micro Science
IAG – Institut d'Administration et de Gestion (UCL) Louvain School of Management (UCL)
IBA – Ion Beam Applications
IIPN – Institut Interuniversitaire de Physique Nucléaire
IISN – Institut Interuniversitaire des Sciences Nucléaires
IMPT – Intensity-Modulated Proton Therapy
IPO – Initial Public Offering
IRE – Institut National des Radioéléments National Institute for Radioelements
keV – kiloelectronvolt
kW – Kilowatt
Linac – Linear Accelerator
LLUMC – Loma Linda University Medical Center
M&A – Mergers and Acquisitions
MeV – Megaelectronvolt
MGH – Massachusetts General Hospital (Boston)
MYRRHA – Multi-purpose hYbrid Research Reactor for High-tech Applications
NASDAQ – National Association of Securities Dealers Automated Quotations
NCI – National Cancer Institute (United States)
NGO – Non-Governmental Organization
NHa – Normandy Hadrontherapy
OKR – Objectives and Key Results
ONDD – Office National du Ducroire (Belgique) / Belgian Export Credit Agency

PBS – Pencil Beam Scanning
PET – Positron Emission Tomography
PFAS – Per- and polyfluoroalkyl substances
PSI – Paul Scherrer Institute (Switzerland)
PTCA – Proton Therapy Corporation of America
PT COG – Particle Therapy Co-Operative Group
R&D – Research and development
RDI – Radiation Dynamics Inc.
S2C2 – Superconducting Synchrocyclotron Project
SCK-CEN – Studiecentrum voor Kernenergie – Centre d'Étude de l'Énergie Nucléaire
Belgian Nuclear Research Centre
SF_6 – Sulfur Hexafluoride
SME – Small and Medium-sized Enterprises
SPECT – Single Photon Emission Computed Tomography
SRIW – Société Régionale d'Investissement de Wallonie / Regional Investment Company of Wallonia
TCC – The Cyclotron Corporation
TPS – Treatment Planning System
UCL – Université Catholique de Louvain
Catholic University of Louvain
UFH – University of Florida Hospital
ULB – Université Libre de Bruxelles
UPenn – University of Pennsylvania
UWE – Union Wallonne des Entreprises

List of interviewees

Michel Abs, Daphnée Benayoun, Jean-Louis Bol, Jean-Marc Bothy, Dominique Bourgeois, Thomas Canon, Renaud Dehareng, Nicolas Denef, Claude Dupont, Daniel Ernult, Henri de Romrée, Micheline Desmedt, Sabine de Voghel, Yves Jongen, Charles Kumps, Serge Lamisse, Olivier Legrain, Stéphane Lucas, Nancy Mendenhall, Astrid Mertens, Marcel Miller, Pierre Mottet, Bruno Scutnaire, Thomas Servais, Françoise Vamecq, Catherine Vandenborre, Sybille van den Hove, Anne-Marie Vranckx.

List of registered trademarks

ConformalFLASH, Cyclone KEY, Cyclone KIUBE, Cyclone IKON, Cyclone 3 / 10 / 11 / 18/9 / 30 / 70 / 230 / 235 / 400, DynamicARC, IntegraLab, ProteusONE, ProteusPLUS, Rhodotron, Synthera

Notes

[1] B. L. Doyle, F. D. McDaniel, and R. Hamm, The Future of Industrial Accelerators and Applications, *Reviews of Accelerator Science and Technology*, 2019, pp. 93-116.
[2] https://cyclotron.lbl.gov/ionsources/ecr (accessed on 06/22/2025).
[3] P. Macq, Marc de Hemptinne, fondateur des cyclotrons de Belgique, *Physicalia Magazine*, 8 n°2, 1986, p. 91 and following.
[4] P. Govaerts, A. Jaumotte, J. Vanderlinden ed., *Un demi-siècle de nucléaire en Belgique. Témoignages*, Presses interuniversitaires européennes, Brussels, 1990.
[5] A. Jaumotte, Le début du nucléaire en Belgique, *Bulletins de l'Académie Royale de Belgique*, 2003, 14-7-2, pp. 245-254.
[6] P. Macq, Le cyclotron isochrone de l'UCL et sa vocation interuniversitaire, *Nouvelles de la science et des technologies*, 3 n°2, 1985, p. 43 and following.
[7] P. Marage, Éléments d'histoire du développement de la physique nucléaire et des particules élémentaires en Belgique, *Histoire des Sciences en Belgique, 1815-2000*, edited by R. Halleux, J. Vandersmissen, A. Despy-Mayer, and G. Vanpaemel, Brussels, 2001, t. II, pp. 85-108.
[8] Approximate maximum speed of a proton accelerated in a 230 MeV cyclotron.
[9] According to the unpublished memoirs of Yves Jongen, 2005.
[10] *Ibidem.*
[11] P. Marage, *Op. Cit.*, p. 101.
[12] J. Vervier, Le Centre de Recherches du Cyclotron de l'U.C.L. à Louvain-la-Neuve : une approche multidisciplinaire de la recherche fondamentale et de la recherche appliquée, *Bulletins de l'Académie Royale de Belgique*, 1996, 7-1-6, pp. 195-221.
[13] IBA Archives, Board Meeting Minutes, December 7, 1988.
[14] The development of microfiltration membranes was entrusted to a separate company, Cyclopore, which later became IT4IP. Wear and tear led to another spin-off, DSI, which is still operating in Mons. The Channel Tunnel security scanning project did not proceed, nor did subsequent drug-detection projects in ports, despite significant efforts, because their costs were too high.
[15] Interview with Yves Jongen.
[16] IBA Archives – Preparatory note for the Board of Directors meeting of June 28, 1991.
[17] Interview with Yves Jongen.
[18] Un cyclotron anticancer, *La Dernière Heure*, March 14, 1993.
[19] IBA Archives, 1994 Business Review, Board of Directors meeting of December 8, 1994.
[20] IBA Archives, 1997 Management Report.
[21] Appointed president of SRIW in 2009, Olivier Vanderijst patiently rebuilt a relationship that made SRIW (which became Wallonie Entreprendre in 2023) IBA's main partner in anchor equity and an attentive co-investor in IBA's joint ventures (Normandy Hadrontherapy, PanTera, MI-2).
[22] Yves Jongen et Pierre Mottet, Managers de l'année, *Trends / Tendances*, January 8, 1998, pp. 18-24.
[23] La confiance du marché est toujours plus facile à gagner qu'à restaurer, *L'Écho*, June 10, 2000.
[24] Interview with Yves Jongen.
[25] IBA archives, minutes of the Board of Directors meetings of March 19, 2002, and September 12, 2002
[26] IBA Archives, minutes of the Board of Directors meeting of December 18, 2003.
[27] IBA Archives, IBA S.A. Preliminary analysis of the implementation of the Belgian Corporate Governance Code, 2004; IBA Corporate Governance Charter, May 2005.
[28] The stakeholder theory was formalized by American economist and philosopher R. Edward Freeman in 1984, based on debates throughout the 20th century about the role

of business in society. It advocates striking a balance between the potentially conflicting interests of an organization's various stakeholders, thereby opposing the purely shareholder-focused approach championed by Milton Friedman, who believed that corporate social responsibility was limited to increasing profits and maximizing shareholder value.
[29] Interview with Jean-Louis Bol.
[30] Interview with Pierre Mottet.
[31] Interview with Dr Nancy Mendenhall.
[32] Interview with Serge Lamisse.
[33] Quote provided by Pierre Mottet.
[34] B. Glimelius, A. Ask, G. Bjelkengren, T. Björk-Eriksson, E. Blomquist, B. Johansson, M. Karlsson, B. Zackrisson, Number of patients potentially eligible for proton therapy, *Acta Oncologica*, 44(8), 2005, pp. 836-49.
[35] IBA Archives, minutes of the Board of Directors meeting of May 12, 2004.
[36] Olivier Legrain, *Du cyclotron de laboratoire à l'entreprise au rayonnement international*, Report on the seminar Industrial Adventures at the Paris School of Management, March 25, 2025.
[37] *Ibidem.*
[38] Interview with Olivier Legrain.
[39] IBA Archives, minutes of the Board of Directors meeting of May 8, 2013.
[40] IBA, Non-Financial Activity Report, 2017.
[41] According to an expression used in the article : La Wallonie débourse 47 millions pour la protonthérapie, *L'Écho*, April 28, 2014.
[42] Interview with Bruno Scutnaire.
[43] According to a phrase used by Olivier Legrain in a presentation to students at the Louvain School of Management in October 2020.
[44] Interview with Olivier Legrain.
[45] P. de Woot, L'entrepreneur, *Reflets et perspectives de la vie économique*, De Boeck Université, Tome XLIV (1), 2005, pp. 93-105.
[46] Unpublished memoirs of Yves Jongen, 2005.
[47] Interview with Dominique Bourgeois.
[48] Collective reflection by the IBA management team.
[49] Archives IBA, Archives du CA, *Organigramme et organisation actuelle d'IBA*, 18 avril 1991.
[50] Speech by Yves Jongen at the Philippe de Woot Award ceremony, 2016.
[51] Interview with Pierre Mottet.
[52] Formulation by Henri de Romrée, during a collective reflection by the management team.
[53] Formulation by Yves Jongen.
[54] Interview with Charles Kumps.
[55] Formulation by Catherine Vandenborre during a collective reflection session with the management team.
[56] Collective reflection by the management team.
[57] Sources: United Nations, *World Population Prospects 2024*; PNUD, *Human Development Report 2023/24*; World Bank, *World Development Indicators*; World Inequality Database; IARC, *GLOBOCAN 2020*; NOAA, *Global Monitoring Laboratory*; IPCC, *Sixth Assessment Report, 2023.*
[58] « Quelles perspectives donne-t-on aux jeunes avec le catastrophisme ? », interview with Olivier Legrain in *L'Écho*, December 22, 2019.
[59] Interview with Marcel Miller.
[60] The royalties from the sale of this book will be donated to the Oncia Community Foundation.
[61] The resale of part of UCL's stake in IBA enabled the university to finance a large part of its Aula Magna auditorium and several other spin-offs.
[62] Interview with Marcel Miller.
[63] Interview with Jean-Louis Bol.

Acknowledgements

I am very grateful to the members of the quartet who initiated and supervised the project—Yves Jongen, Pierre Mottet, Olivier Legrain, and Henri de Romrée—for trusting me with the task of researching and transcribing the history and philosophy of IBA. Their open-mindedness and dedication to transparency and pedagogy allowed me to carry out my research and write this book. Alongside them, around thirty employees, administrators, and clients generously shared their insights with me as firsthand witnesses to this entrepreneurial adventure. Although I haven't named them all, each contributed to this project. I want to especially thank Marie Gahylle and Giulia Marino for their invaluable logistical, organizational, and legal support, as well as Daniel Ernult for researching and selecting the illustrations. A big thank you to my dearest Marie, Caroline, and Nadine for their meticulous proofreading, and to Victoria and Noah for their support with documentary research. This book was made possible by the efficient and friendly collaboration of Michelle Poskin, editor-in-chief of Éditions Racine.
It was beautifully designed by Dominique Hambÿe and carefully translated from French into English by Paula Cook.

Nicolas Coupain

Author **Nicolas Coupain**
Graphic design and layout
Dominique Hambÿe
Translation **Paula Cook**
Proofreading **Textcase** textcase.com

Royalties from the sale of the books will be donated to the Oncia Community Foundation > https://oncia-community.org/

The cover photo was kindly provided by the Mommaerts family.

All photographs are from the IBA collection except pages 22–23. © The Regents of the University of California, Lawrence Berkeley National Laboratory and page 167, X. Ding, X. Li, J.-M. Zhang, P. Kabolizadeh, C. Stevens, D. Yan, "Spot-Scanning Proton Arc (SPArc) Therapy: The First Robust and Delivery-Efficient Spot-Scanning Proton Arc Therapy", in *International journal of radiation oncology, biology, physics*, 1 Dec 2016 ; 96(5):1107-1116.

Éditions Racine / Lannoo Publishers
https://www.lannoopublishers.com/en
Tour & Taxis – Entrepôt royal
Avenue du Port, 86C / bte 104A
B-1000 Brussels
Tel. +32 (0)2 646 44 44
www.racine.be

ISBN 978-23-902-5388-4
Legal deposit D/2025/6852/8
Printed in Europe